The Geller Phenomenon

The Geller Phenomenon

by Colin Wilson

Aldus Books London

Series Coordinator: John Mason
Design Director: Gunter Radtke
Picture Editor: Peter Cook
Editor: Eleanor Van Zandt
Copy Editor: Maureen Cartwright
Research: Frances Vargo
General Consultant: Beppie Harrison

EDITORIAL CONSULTANTS:

COLIN WILSON
DR. CHRISTOPHER EVANS

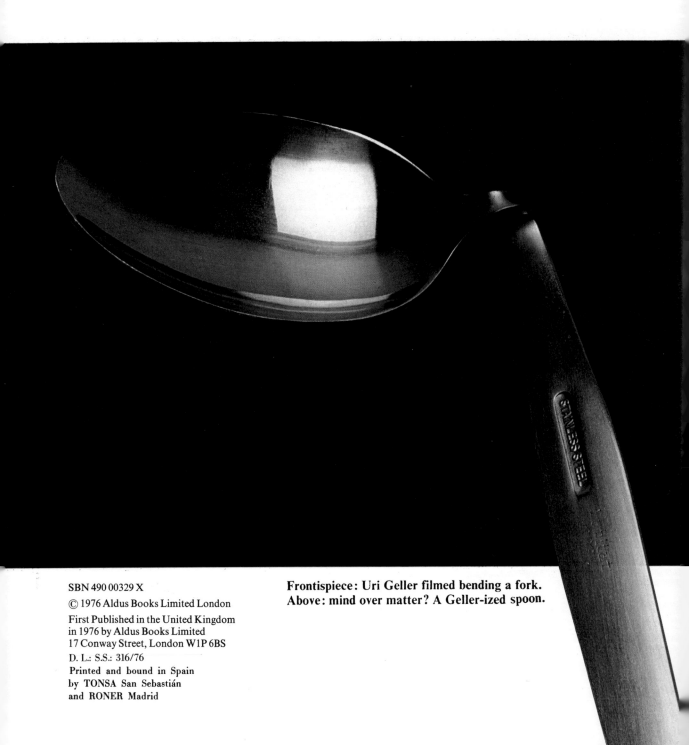

SBN 490 00329 X

© 1976 Aldus Books Limited London

First Published in the United Kingdom
in 1976 by Aldus Books Limited
17 Conway Street, London W1P 6BS

D. L.: S.S.: 316/76

Printed and bound in Spain
by TONSA San Sebastián
and RONER Madrid

**Frontispiece: Uri Geller filmed bending a fork.
Above: mind over matter? A Geller-ized spoon.**

The Geller Phenomenon

One of the most controversial of modern writers here examines one of the most controversial of modern phenomena – the young Israeli psychic Uri Geller. Writers and scientists are sharply divided over the seemingly miraculous feats Geller performs. Now Colin Wilson weighs up the evidence and offers his own balanced interpretation.

Contents

1

The Making of a Mystic

In the spring of 1974, publishers in Britain and the United States announced the forthcoming appearance of a book by the well-known scientist and parapsychologist, Dr. Andrija Puharich. The title alone was enough to bring a gleam of anticipation into the eyes of booksellers—*Uri: A Journal of the Mystery of Uri Geller*. Uri Geller was the young Israeli psychic who had achieved overnight fame less than a year before with his remarkable feats of telepathy, and by his even more baffling ability to bend spoons and repair broken watches by merely touching them. On subsequent trips around Europe and America, he had become a subject of inter-

Most people like to have the world behave in a broadly predictable fashion: a phenomenon such as Uri Geller, which seems to upset normal expectations, arouses a peculiar mixture of fascination and hostility.
Right: Uri Geller, with one of the thousands of keys he has bent during his spectacular career.

"Suddenly, the scholar went into a trance"

national controversy. And in these days when any book on an occult subject has a ready market, both the subject and the title of Puharich's biography promised a best seller.

In due course, the book made its appearance. But the anticipated rush never happened. Puharich had apparently achieved the impossible: he had written a book that was so astonishing and unbelievable that nobody wanted to read it. Even the reviews were muted, as if reviewers felt that Puharich had played an unfair trick. He was known as a respectable scientist; the writer Aldous Huxley had described him as "one of the most brilliant minds in parapsychology"; his book *Beyond Telepathy* had become a classic of scientific investigation. Yet contact with the young Israeli seemed to have destroyed his judgment. He was actually asserting that Uri Geller was some kind of divine messenger, an instrument of "the controllers of the universe," and that the aim of these mysterious entities was to bring a new age of peace and prosperity to the earth. Everyone had been expecting a book about carefully planned experiments, and perhaps some bold and original theory about psychic energies. All this stuff about spaceships and extraterrestrials was a bit too much.

To do Puharich justice, the book was less bizarre than it sounded. *If* the events he described were true, then his conclusions were logical enough, if a trifle incautious. For his story, in brief, was as follows:

In 1952, Puharich had been investigating a Hindu scholar who possessed clairvoyant powers. Suddenly, the scholar went into a trance, and proceeded to speak in a strange voice, with a perfect English accent. The voice described itself as a representative of "the Nine Principles and Forces," superhuman intelligences whose aim is to aid human evolution.

Four years later, in Mexico, Puharich met a doctor and his wife who had also been in touch with "Space Beings," through the mouth of a trance medium. Some time later, this doctor sent Puharich two "messages" he had received from the Space Beings, who had ordered him to transmit them to Puharich. The messages stated that they were the same "Nine Principles" who had spoken through the Hindu scholar, and that they would be contacting Puharich again in due course. Puharich naturally suspected that the doctor had somehow found out about his earlier sessions with the Hindu scholar. But this, apparently, was not so.

In the 1960s, Puharich became fascinated by the strange feats of the Brazilian "psychic surgeon" Arigó. This man, an ordinary mine worker, had one day gone into a trance, seized a knife, and performed a surgical operation on a woman who was dying. The operation—done without anesthetic or sterilization—had been completely successful. Arigó set up a surgery and performed hundreds of such operations. The operations were usually performed with a rusty kitchen knife, which Arigó wiped on his shirt to clean it. The wounds never turned septic, and they healed without the help of antibiotics or germicides. There is no record of any failures. Arigó attributed these astonishing feats to the spirit of a dead German surgeon who, he claimed, possessed him while he was in a trance. Puharich visited Arigó and observed his work, and Arigó successfully removed a tumor from Puharich's forearm. But in January 1971, Arigó was killed in a car crash.

Puharich was stricken with guilt, feeling that he should have devoted all his time to investigating this remarkable man while he was still alive.

At the time Arigó was killed, Puharich had already read a report about a young Israeli with incredible powers, including the ability to move the hands of a watch without touching it, and to cause a ring—held by someone else—to snap, merely by cupping his hands around the person's hand. Puharich resolved that this time he would not fail. He wrote to Uri Geller in Israel and went to see him. In due course, he brought Geller to America. One day, when Geller was in a light hypnotic trance, a strange metallic voice speaking from the air identified itself as some kind of superhuman (or nonhuman) entity, and went on to explain that

Above: Andrija Puharich, American doctor and parapsychologist, who has an established reputation as a sound researcher in the field of paranormal claims and activities. He was the first international figure to take a scientific interest in Geller's achievements.

9

Above: José Arigó, the Brazilian psychic surgeon, who died in 1971. His sudden death was a great blow to Puharich, who was overwhelmed with a sense of lost opportunities. He resolved that should he ever find another equally gifted psychic he would not fail again.

"they" had chosen Geller to be an instrument of their purpose. In later communications, the Space Beings identified themselves as the Nine—of whom Puharich had heard for the first time some 20 years earlier—and explained that they existed in another dimension, outside space and time, and had been watching the human race for some thousands of years. At present, they were in a "starship" called *Spectra* somewhere out in space. They were connected with the phenomena we know as "flying saucers" or UFOs. Their ultimate purpose was to save man from destroying himself, and to bring world peace.

The metallic voice was not, apparently, the real voice of the Space Being; it was created electronically. Puharich tape-recorded it, but the tapes were always mysteriously wiped. Photographs of UFOs taken by Geller and Puharich failed to develop, or vanished. But the extraterrestrials periodically proved their powers by such feats as stopping a car engine and restarting it, and transporting Puharich's briefcase from America to Israel.

No wonder the critics were baffled, astonished, and in some cases outraged. The simplest hypotheses were that Puharich had gone insane, or was telling lies. A typical review, by D. Scott Rogo, a writer on psychic phenomena, pointed out that Puharich expects the reader to take his word for all kinds of absurdities without offering evidence for a single one of them. The vanishing photographs and tape messages were really rather convenient, Rogo observed. As to the claim that Uri had been chosen as the unique "messenger" of these Space Beings, it can be undermined by simply glancing at the list of books by "contactees"—people who claim to have been inside flying saucers or to have spoken to their inhabitants. There is not a single claim in the whole book, says Rogo, that can stand up to serious examination.

All of which is obviously true. Yet it apparently solves one problem only to leave another just as baffling. If Puharich is a liar, why is he such a bad liar? If he wanted to advance Geller's claims as the world's most extraordinary psychic, all he had to do was to write a detailed account of the experiments he had carried out under controlled conditions. Some of these—such as the ability to dematerialize small animals and transport them to other places—were astounding enough on their own. The stuff about *Spectra* simply isn't necessary. And even if Puharich was cunning enough to anticipate this reaction and hope that people would mistake his lack of solid evidence for honesty, the book still wouldn't advance Geller's case—as, in fact, it didn't.

Besides, Puharich's integrity as an investigator of the paranormal had already been proved by his remarkable first book, *The Sacred Mushroom*. In it, he describes his investigations of a young Dutch sculptor named Harry Stone, who periodically went into trances, spoke ancient Egyptian, and wrote Egyptian hieroglyphs. The "trance personality" who spoke through Stone claimed to be an Egyptian of the Fourth Dynasty named Ra Ho Tep. Puharich spent three years studying the ancient Egyptian language and hieroglyphs and diligently trying to find some historical record of the original Ra Ho Tep. His summing-up of the evidence about Harry Stone is a model of scientific caution and lucidity, demonstrating that he understood—and thoroughly accepted—the scientist's obligation to be tough-minded. The

same quality is apparent in his book *Beyond Telepathy*, in which, after citing many cases of telepathy, apparitions, and "astral travel" (the experience of being outside one's body), he calls upon the aid of modern physics and mathematics to attempt to establish the existence of "psi plasma." He explains how this psi plasma (which the layman could translate as "mind stuff") can operate between human minds to produce psychic phenomena. No one who has read these two books could believe for one moment that Puharich is secretly a cranky "occultist" masquerading as a scientist.

All of which leaves us with the disturbing question: Could Puharich be right? Are there really "super beings" who have been observing our earth for thousands of years, and who have chosen Uri Geller as a "transmitter" because his biological make-up happens to be appropriate? Or could there be some other explanation of the mystery that we have not so far considered?

Before we examine these questions more fully, let us turn our attention to the career of the man at the heart of the controversy: Uri Geller.

Geller is a Hungarian name, and Uri's parents, Itzhaak and Margaret, had fled from Hungary shortly before the Second World War. They succeeded in reaching Palestine (now Israel) in 1940. Itzhaak Geller joined the British Army, and fought against Rommel's forces in North Africa. Uri was born on December 20, 1946, in Tel Aviv. His parents' marriage began to break up when his father fell in love with another woman.

When I questioned Uri about the origin of his powers, he mentioned an incident to which he attached little importance—so little that he had not even bothered to mention it to other interviewers. His mother had a sewing machine, which had a small

Above: Geller with Puharich. In 1971 Puharich came to Israel to find out more about Geller, whose fame was beginning to spread outside his own country. He was greatly impressed, and persuaded him to cooperate with scientific research into his strange powers.

hole through which he could see a tiny blue spark. One day, when he was five years old, he tried to touch the spark with his finger; the shock threw him backward violently.

Oddly enough, his powers began to manifest themselves at about this time. He discovered one day that he could read his mother's mind. When she came back from playing cards with friends, he suddenly knew precisely how much money she had lost. She was astounded when he named the exact figure. He also noticed that he would often start to say things at the same moment that she did. This kind of thing is not, of course, unusual. Many married couples have the same experience of telepathic contact, and it is not uncommon between parents and young children. (When my own children were babies, I could wake them up merely by thinking about them.)

The tangible phenomena began when he was six. His father had given him a watch. One day, in class, he noticed that it was half an hour fast. There was nothing very odd about that; he put it right. When it happened several more times, he decided there was something wrong with the watch. When left at home, it behaved perfectly. Then one day he placed it in front of him on the desk and saw that the hands were going around much too fast. Deciding it was faulty, he persuaded his parents to buy him another, but its hands somehow bent upward so that they pressed against the glass; it was ruined. Some time later, as he sat in class without a watch, the boy sitting next to him remarked: "My watch just moved on an hour." In a mischievous mood, Uri said, "I did that." He took the watch, concentrated on it, and somehow made the hands move ahead. Uri gained a reputation among his schoolfriends.

Then the spoon bending began. One day while he was eating soup, the bowl of the spoon fell off the handle. In a coffee shop that he sometimes frequented with his mother, the spoons began bending although he was not touching them. His father thought of taking him to see a psychiatrist, but later dropped the idea.

That may be a pity. An open-minded psychiatrist would have recognized that these phenomena *could* be due to some paranormal forces. (Of course, he would first have had to satisfy himself that Uri was not faking the occurrences to get attention.) And if the psychiatrist had any kind of interest in the paranormal phenomena, he might also have decided that they were worth investigating. By 1955 (when the spoon bending started), it was common knowledge that so-called "poltergeist" phenomena are often caused spontaneously by emotionally disturbed children and adolescents.

Uri's home life was certainly insecure at this time—his father was always disappearing with the "other woman." So poltergeist phenomena would have been a sensible hypothesis. Uri's strange powers might have been investigated some 15 years before they came to the attention of Andrija Puharich. Whether this would have shed any more light on them than we have at the moment is a matter for speculation.

When his parents finally divorced, Uri was sent to a kibbutz near Tel Aviv. He was lonely there, and was glad when his mother got married again—this time to a Hungarian pianist—and told

Above left: Uri with his mother, when he was about two years old. By this time, in 1948, his parents had escaped separately from the Nazis and made their way to Israel.

Right: Geller at school in Nicosia, Cyprus, in 1963. He was now attending a Roman Catholic school on a hill overlooking the city. At the school he discovered he could use his telepathic powers deliberately: once he summoned help when he was lost, and often he read the mind of a more clever pupil during class examinations.

him they were all moving to Cyprus. There, as in Israel, Uri was again surrounded by war: the conflict between Greek and Turkish Cypriots. In Cyprus he used his powers deliberately for the first time. In the family's garage was a bicycle that his stepfather had promised him as a Bar Mitzvah present. It was secured by a combination lock. Uri was eager to try the bicycle, so one day he concentrated hard on the lock and willed it to open. After several attempts, it suddenly gave way. Having obtained his present, the boy taught himself to ride.

One day Uri's stepfather had a heart attack. Unaware of this, Uri experienced an odd compulsion to go to the hospital, and actually found his way to the room where his mother sat beside his stepfather's bed. We may surmise that he had been "guided in" telepathically by his mother. The telepathic link between them was as strong as ever; he tells how, when she was in an auto accident in Haifa, he knew about it at the moment it happened,

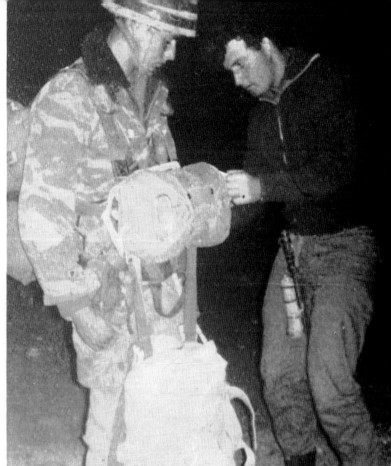

Above: Geller with his father in 1967. At that time Uri was a paratrooper, and his father was a sergeant major in the Tank Corps.

Above right: Geller's parachute being checked by the instructor before he made a night jump.

although he was himself in Tel Aviv and several hours elapsed before he was able to verify it.

In Cyprus, Uri was sent to a Roman Catholic school, which he disliked. While he was there an incident occurred that suggested he could send, as well as receive, telepathic messages. In defiance of school rules, the boys used to explore the deep caves in the hills near the school. One day Uri ventured too far into a cave and lost his way. He sat down in the dark and prayed. An hour later, he heard a bark. The family dog had come out from Nicosia, 10 miles away, and found its way through the cave to Uri. They played together for a while, and then the dog led him safely out of the cave.

Uri soon discovered that his telepathic faculties were useful in exams. He only had to stare at the back of the head of a clever pupil to see the answers to questions. (He describes the sensation as being like a television screen inside his own head.) Teachers suspected him of cheating, because he got the other pupil's mistakes as well as his correct answers, and they moved Uri to a distant corner of the room. Distance made no difference; he still got the answers—and the mistakes. The teachers may have begun to suspect that something strange was going on when Uri began bending keys and mending watches by resting his hand on them. Years later, one of them, Mrs. Julie Agrotis, wrote a letter to the British newspaper *News of the World*, confirming that Uri's spoon-bending feats had already begun while he was at school. The period at the Catholic school came to an end when his step-father died of a heart attack.

It was while he was in Cyprus that Uri became involved with the Israeli Intelligence Service. He discovered that a friend named Joav was an Israeli spy. Joav agreed to let the boy help by serving as a courier there in Nicosia. This work came to an end when Uri's family returned to Tel Aviv. Uri went into the Israeli Army as a paratrooper to do his military service. It was while on maneuvers with the paras that he had his strangest experience up to that time. It was his job to carry a heavy Browning machine gun. Because he had no expectation of using it on the first day of maneuvers, he decided to leave behind the heavy parts of the gun, including the barrel and firing pin. Then, unexpectedly, they were ordered to open fire on an imaginary enemy. Thinking quickly, Uri placed a small gun beside the stripped-down Browning and hoped that no one would notice that the big gun was not working. But when he pressed the trigger of the small gun, both guns started firing. An officer congratulated him on his shooting. The Browning was surrounded by its empty cartridge cases. It had fired without a barrel or firing pin.

In 1967 war broke out between Israel and Egypt—the Six Day War. Uri had a premonition that he would be badly hurt, but not killed. It proved to be correct: he was injured by a grenade, and his arms, legs, and forehead were peppered with shrapnel. While he was recuperating, he was offered a job in a children's holiday camp near Tel Aviv. There he met a boy called Shipi, who was to become one of his closest friends. Shipi persuaded him to put on a demonstration of his powers, for a fee, at his school. It was Uri's first public performance. It lasted for two hours and included

Below: Uri with one of his friends who was wounded near him in the Six Day War in 1967. He sensed beforehand that he would be injured himself, but fortunately his own injuries were not serious.

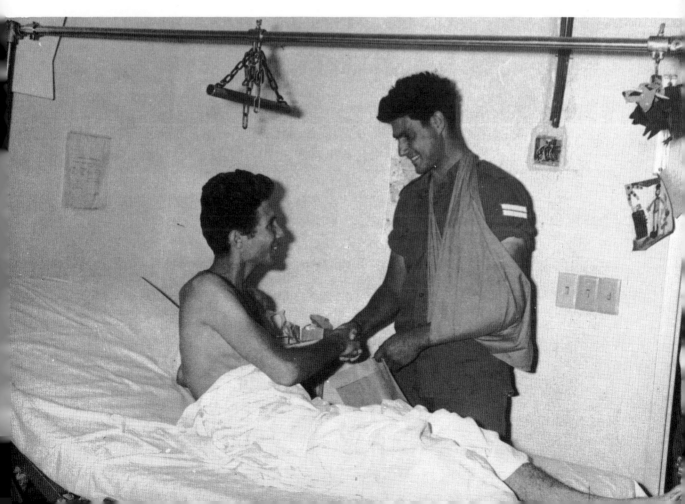

his now familiar feats of mind reading, watch repairing, and spoon bending. It was a great success.

When he came out of the Army, in 1968, Uri continued giving shows while he tried to make up his mind what to do with his future. One day it dawned on him that he could make a living by continuing with his demonstrations. Soon he was sufficiently well known to be signed on by a professional manager. And here he made his first crucial mistake: he allowed the manager to persuade him to cheat. Of course, in the context of professional stage magic it was not cheating to use perfectly normal means to discover, for example, the license plate number of somebody's car, and then to pretend to have discovered it by mind reading. But for someone claiming genuine psychic powers, to resort to occasional trickery can seriously undermine his reputation if he is found out.

Around this time, Uri's life began to go sour. An appearance in Rome proved a flop. There was a small scandal about a composite photograph of Uri with Sophia Loren. The photo had been faked by a photographer who had not been allowed to take a picture when Uri visited the film star in Italy. Although Uri had nothing to do with organizing the deception, it created a bad impression.

In 1970, Uri met an Israeli psychical researcher named Itzhaak Bentov, who worked in America. For Bentov, he demonstrated his ability to break metal—in this case, a pin—while it was held in someone else's hand. Bentov sent the two broken halves of the pin to Andrija Puharich in America. As a result, Puharich came to Israel to meet Geller. It was to be a turning point in Uri's career.

Puharich met Uri Geller in a Jaffa discotheque on August 17, 1971. After being introduced, Puharich sat in the audience, and listened to a succession of pop singers, clowns, and comedians. Geller then came on stage—the youthful audience cheering wildly—and announced that he would attempt to demonstrate telepathy and psychokinesis. The telepathy consisted of the usual mind-reading act: Geller was blindfolded, and then accurately "guessed" various words written on a blackboard by members of the audience. After this, he broke a ring held in a woman's hand by cupping his own hands around hers. Puharich later admitted thinking at the time that the effects were probably produced by trickery.

But a series of tests in Puharich's own private apartment the following day led him to change his opinion. Geller wrote a number on a sheet of paper, then asked Puharich to think of three figures. When Puharich had done so, he was shown the paper: Geller had written the same three figures *before* Puharich thought of them. He had apparently made Puharich think of them by transmitting them telepathically. During this and subsequent sessions, Geller performed other feats under Puharich's close observation. He started a watch that had deliberately been allowed to run down—without touching it—and caused a wedding ring to crack while it was being held in someone else's clenched hand.

Now Puharich was totally convinced that Geller's gift was no fake. In the first of a series of tests involving scientific instruments,

Left: after the war and his army service, Uri began to do some lecture demonstrations of his powers. The poster at his shoulder announces one such demonstration.

Right: Geller with a sign forbidding left turns that bent while he was recording his album at a nearby studio. Later he used this picture for the official autograph photo he sends out to his fans.

Below: Geller with Shipi Shtrang, whom he first met in a children's camp just after the war in 1967. Shipi persuaded Uri to make his first public appearance, and now helps manage his business life.

Geller raised the mercury in a thermometer six to eight degrees Fahrenheit apparently by willing it to rise, while the mercury in a second thermometer nearby remained unaffected.

Asked by Puharich if he had any theory that might explain his powers, Uri suggested that perhaps telepathy acts at a greater speed than light—which, according to Einstein, is the maximum attainable speed in our universe—and that this might explain how the laws of nature were apparently being broken. He also hazarded the guess that he might be the descendant of "space men" who possessed great powers and who landed on earth a long time ago. Von Däniken's *Chariots of the Gods?* had been published in English some two years before, not long after the release of Stanley Kubrick's well-known film *2001: A Space*

An early Geller stage performance in Geneva, Switzerland. Skeptics and believers alike agree that Geller is a natural showman. He wrote himself of his very first performance, at a school, that he "was fascinated with the reaction of the audience and gratified by the interest of both teachers and children." That first show, like this one in Geneva, was an immediate and complete success.

Odyssey; and so the idea was very much in the air at the time.

The most extraordinary session took place on December 1, 1971. This was the occasion when the computerlike voice spoke from the air. But before this happened, Geller was placed in a hypnotic trance, and asked a number of questions about his childhood. He spoke in Hebrew (because he had not learned English until he moved to Cyprus), and described his early years in Tel Aviv. And then, suddenly, he told an extraordinary story. At the age of three, he had gone into a garden opposite his home. In the sky above his head, he noticed a bright, bowl-shaped object. There was a high-pitched ringing sound in the air. The light came down closer, dazzling him, so that he fell to the ground and lost consciousness.

Puharich quotes two versions of this story in his book *Uri*; in both of them, he mentions that some kind of figure, with a shining face, appeared in front of the child, and that a ray of light emanating from its head knocked Uri to the ground. In Geller's own version, in his autobiography *My Story*, there was no mysterious figure. The child was simply dazzled by the light of the bowl, and felt as if he had been knocked over backward. This version certainly sounds less incredible than the one Puharich relates.

It was after Geller had told his story of the garden, on tape, that the metallic voice issued from the air, explaining that "we" (the Nine) had found Uri in the garden when he was three (Puharich gives the exact date—December 25, 1949), and decided that his biological make-up was suitable for their purposes: that is, he was a suitable "receiving station" for the powers they would

Below: in Germany in 1972. His new manager suggested that Uri might try a few spectacular experiments, to give his series of lecture demonstrations a good launching in the press with a lot of publicity. One such stunt was to try to stop this escalator in a large Munich department store. Uri and his party traveled on the store's escalator for about 20 trips before the escalator stopped dead—as much to Geller's surprise as to anyone else's.

transmit through him. "We reveal ourselves because we believe that man may be on the threshold of a world war. Plans for war have been made by Egypt, and if Israel loses, the whole world will explode into war."

When Uri awoke from his hypnotic trance, the tape was played back to him. He recalled nothing of what had taken place, and when his own voice related the garden episode, he commented: "I don't remember any of this." When the metallic voice started, Geller reached out, removed the cassette from the recorder, paused for a moment with the cassette in his hand, then rushed out of the room. Puharich says that the tape vanished as Geller's hand closed over it. He was found later standing in an empty elevator, apparently in a state of shock. The tape was not recovered.

This was the first of a series of strange events that give Puharich's book the quality of a surrealistic nightmare. There were more messages from "the Nine"—although the tapes were found to be wiped blank when they were played back later. Sometimes the cassette recorder itself "spoke," with the recording key depressed by some invisible force, but nothing was heard on the tape when it was played back. In the desert, in an army jeep (Uri had been entertaining troops), Puharich and Geller saw a red light that they took to be a flying saucer; the soldiers driving the jeep saw nothing. An army cap that one of the soldiers had left on his bed appeared on Puharich's head. A ballpoint pen with an especially numbered cartridge was placed in a sealed box, and when the box was opened a few minutes later, the cartridge had vanished from the pen. Soon afterward, Geller experienced an urge to take Puharich to a suburb of Tel Aviv at night; there they saw a "ball of pulsating bluish-white light" on a deserted lot.

Geller approached it, seemed to go into a kind of trance, and returned holding the cartridge from the ballpoint pen.

In February 1972, Puharich was about to leave Israel for Rome when Israeli Intelligence officers insisted on searching him. They confiscated various films, books, and letters. It seemed that they were convinced Puharich was some kind of superspy. (This incident may have been related to Uri's former spy-ring connections.) On his arrival in Rome, Puharich contacted New York and heard that people were saying he had gone insane, and that Geller was his evil genius. Puharich decided it was time to relax for a while; he found a remote hotel on top of a mountain pass, and began to write his book about Uri Geller.

Meanwhile, back in Israel, Uri accepted an offer to appear in Germany. The man who arranged the tour understood the value of publicity; when Uri and his friend Shipi arrived, they were met by crowds of reporters and batteries of cameras. A Munich newspaper ran a six-part series about him. In answer to his manager's plea that he try something spectacular, Uri apparently stopped a cable car on the side of a mountain and an escalator in a Munich department store. It is possible that both these events were coincidence—both the escalator and the cable car had worked for some time before his efforts to stop them had any effect. And skeptics were not slow to point out that the newspaper in question had a certain interest in the project, and that a bribe of a few hundred marks could have stopped the escalator and the cable car as effectively as Geller's supposed supernormal powers. This time, the controversy did Uri no harm. By the time he returned to Israel, and prepared to take off again for America, for a series of controlled tests, he was well on his way to becoming the most famous "psychic" in the world.

2

The Debunking

In spite of his success in Germany, it was to be another year before Uri Geller found his feet firmly planted on the ladder of world fame. The decisive event was his appearance on November 23, 1973 on a British Broadcasting Corporation television program, the "David Dimbleby Talk-In." Also present in the studio were John Taylor, a physicist and professor of mathematics at London University, and biologist Lyall Watson, whose book *Supernature* was on the best seller lists.

Geller was not entirely unknown in Britain. Word had circulated of tests that had been conducted on him at the Stanford Research Institute in California earlier the

"The success had surpassed everyone's expectations, including Geller's"

Below: Geller's most spectacular success came in Britain, where he appeared on a BBC-TV program, the "David Dimbleby Talk-In," a show that dealt with miscellaneous topics in a studio format with an audience present. One program was devoted to Geller, who astonished them. In a telepathy experiment, a sailboat was a target drawing. Below it is Geller's reproduction.

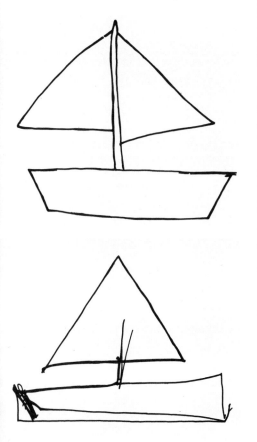

same year, and on several nationwide TV programs, including the Jack Paar show, that he had appeared on. But for some reason Geller's feats had not generated much excitement in the United States. Perhaps the profusion of television stations—as contrasted with the three channels available in most parts of Britain—siphoned off a large proportion of viewers. Or perhaps the presentation of his talents on the American shows was relatively unconvincing. Such attention as he did attract tended to be unfavorable. *Time* magazine, for example, denounced him as a cheat. So the American tour had been anything but an unalloyed success.

The Dimbleby program changed all that. On the table in the BBC studio were various articles, mostly spoons and watches. Geller was handed a sealed envelope, which contained a drawing that had been made immediately before the program. Geller closed his eyes, concentrated on the envelope, and then made a drawing on a sketchpad of a child's sailboat. The envelope was opened and the drawing found to be practically identical to the one Geller had made. Next, David Dimbleby held a fork in his hand, his fingers around its thinnest point, where the handle joins the base. Geller stroked it gently without, apparently, applying any pressure. Within 30 seconds, the fork had begun to bend. Uri later pointed out that another fork that had remained on the table had begun to bend of its own accord. He took watches that had ceased to work, rubbed them gently, and made them start again. Lyall Watson's own watch stopped during this performance. But what probably impressed the audience—and the two scientists—most was that the hands of one of the watches were found to have bent upward so that they pressed on the glass. If this was a conjuring trick—as some of the audience believed— it was difficult to see how he had tampered with a sealed watch.

One member of the audience stood up and said that he would be convinced if Geller could bend a stout metal bar, which he offered to bring onto the platform. Uri declined, explaining that although he *could* do it, it would take so long that the program would be over before he succeeded.

The producer of the program came on to say that they had received dozens of telephone calls from people who said that their own cutlery had been bending while they watched the program or that long-inert watches and clocks had started.

The next morning, Uri was famous. I had missed the program, but someone told me about it before the morning was over. There could be no doubt that the success had surpassed everyone's expectations, including Geller's. On the previous evening, Geller had performed similar feats on a radio program; but then hearing is not the same thing as seeing. Everyone who had watched the "David Dimbleby Talk-In" felt they had personal proof that Geller was genuine. And they wanted to know how he did it. Not next year or next month, but instantly. And because no one knew the answer, it was discussed in pubs, bingo halls, and bowling alleys all over the country. Stage magicians dismissed it scornfully as sleight of hand; one journalist stated authoritatively that he had supervised the preparation of a chemical that would cause metal to crumble and bend, but later had to retract his rash statement. The science editor of the *Sunday*

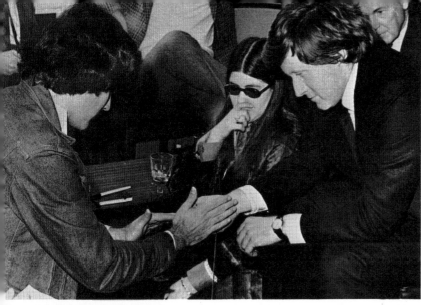

Left: Geller with Dimbleby. In this experiment, Dimbleby held a key ring and key in his palm, and Geller placed his hand over it.

Below left: then Geller took the key ring from Dimbleby and held it in plain view, and the key slowly bent before their eyes.

Below: Dimbleby with his key, now rendered completely useless.

Above: while Geller and Dimbleby were experimenting with the key, London journalist Rosamund Mann was looking on with fascination. (She can be seen in the picture above, next to Dimbleby.) Abruptly, with no warning, a link of her bracelet shattered, and the gold-leaf chain slipped to the floor, surprising all those present.

Below: one of the many cartoons that have appeared about Uri. This one, by Mac, came out at the time of his London success. The caption to it read, "So I said to this guy Uri back there, 'Okay, Smarty-pants, what else can you do, apart from bend spoons?'"

Times, Brian Silcock, described how he had accompanied Uri in a taxi to Heathrow Airport, and offered him his own front door key. As soon as Uri began to stroke it, it bent, so that it was later unusable. Silcock, who had been a skeptic, admitted that he was converted.

When the news of Geller's British triumph reached the United States, the Americans were puzzled and intrigued. Although seemingly more skeptical than the British on Geller's first appearance, they could not help being impressed once he had achieved success abroad. When he returned to the States—and to the anxious scrutiny of Andrija Puharich—Geller found that his rather dubious notoriety had changed into celebrity.

Meanwhile, in England Geller's fame continued to grow in his absence. There were extraordinary reports that during his broadcasts large numbers of the BBC's transmission devices ceased to function. A mass-circulation newspaper, the *Sunday People*, cashed in on the publicity to organize an experiment at short notice: at half past noon on the Sunday following his Friday-evening Dimbleby broadcast, Uri was to concentrate on England (he was at Orly Airport, near Paris, at the time) and order as many spoons as possible to bend. The *People*'s vast readership was asked to cooperate by keeping a careful eye on all cutlery and clocks at this time. The results, published in the following week's edition, included nearly 300 forks and spoons bending and more than 1000 watches or clocks restarting.

But by far the most significant thing about the British success was that scientists took Geller seriously. If he could really read minds and bend spoons, then it ought to be possible to study these phenomena in the laboratory. Of course, Geller had already been tested in America; but that was by scientists specializing in parapsychology. In England, scientists in more orthodox fields, such as Professor John Taylor and Dr. Ted Bastin, both mathematicians, wanted to test Uri in their own laboratories. When the Stanford Institute's report finally appeared, it was in the British

Above and right: Geller with a paper knife at Heathrow Airport, as he was leaving London in 1973. Just before this he had impressed the previously skeptical *Sunday Times* science editor, Brian Silcock, by managing to bend the journalist's own front door key.

journal *Nature*, possibly the most highly regarded scientific journal in the world.

While the publicity continued, and the arguments grew acrimonious, the cause of all the uproar made his way around the world in a leisurely fashion, pausing in Scandinavia, Spain, Italy, and Japan to demonstrate his powers. In Oslo, Geller had just remarked to a reporter that sometimes his psychic energies caused the lights to fuse when suddenly all the street lamps went out. While at sea in the Mediterranean, Geller jokingly asked a few friends to help him to concentrate on stopping the ship. A few minutes later, it slowed down, then stopped. A crimped fuel pipe was later discovered to be the cause. As in the case of the Munich escalator and cable car, both of these curious events could

Left: Geller with Merv Griffin on his talk show in July 1973. On this show everything worked. With Johnny Carson, perhaps because Geller was excited and tense, the results were not so good.

Below: Geller during an impressive 90-minute performance on television in Finland, following his London success with Dimbleby.

have been coincidental. But they made such excellent copy that journalists had no hesitation in writing about them as attested examples of Uri's psychic powers.

Inevitably, the reaction began to set in. Geller himself was undoubtedly shocked and dismayed by it. He found it incomprehensible that he should arouse such violent hostility in people who had never set eyes on him. He remarks, in *My Story*: "I tried not to be on the defensive all the time, but it was sometimes hard."

Yet Geller himself, with his own obsession with fame, should have understood the hostility. It was the normal working of the antisuccess mechanism. In our overcrowded modern world a hit record, a best-selling book, a successful film, can reach more people in a week than Shakespeare or Beethoven reached in a whole lifetime. And so fame has become the most romantic, the most desirable of all commodities, the dream for which a modern Faust might sell his soul to the Devil. Once attained, fame is never as easy to hold on to as most people believe. The people who achieve fame by some accident of fashion are usually forgotten within a week; the ones who remain on top have to work to stay there. But few people understand this. The result is that anyone who achieves sudden notoriety arouses envy and hostility. The greater the success, the greater the reaction. Uri was no longer merely the favorite of some Israeli teenagers in a Tel Aviv discotheque; everything he did now reached an audience of millions. The reaction, when it came, would be on the same scale.

And because America is more success-conscious than most countries, it was inevitable that it should happen there first. In fact, the first shots had already been fired in that country some six months before Geller went to England. *Time* magazine had asked Geller to come to the office for an interview. Also present at the interview were the magician James Randi ("the Amazing Randi") and Charles Reynolds, editor of *Popular Photography* and himself an amateur conjurer. Puharich describes the atmosphere as being that of a kangaroo court. In these hostile surroundings, Geller's psychic powers worked badly; his telepathy demonstrations were fairly successful, but attempts to bend a key and a fork produced little. The *Time* story, which appeared in the second week of March 1973, was a scathing, all-out attack on Geller. It stated that Ray Hyman, a professor of psychology from Oregon, "caught Geller in some outright deceptions." These, apparently, were as follows:

Left: early in 1974 Uri was in Norway, giving another demonstration of his spoon-bending prowess. Here scientist Per Kofstad holds a spoon that Geller touches.
Right: the spoon snaps in two.

Geller asked George Lawrence, a Department of Defense consultant, to think of a number between one and 10 and to write it down, as large as possible, on a notepad. The notepad, of course, was turned away from Geller. But, says the *Time* report, Hyman was able to observe Geller peeking through his fingers, so that he was able "to see the motion of Lawrence's arm as he wrote," and thus correctly guess the number. The other "deception" was practiced when Geller deflected a compass needle by five degrees; Lawrence concluded that it had been done by causing the floor to vibrate, and he repeated the demonstration, causing the needle to deflect even more than five degrees.

Anyone who thinks that one's arm moves while writing a number on a notepad should try the experiment. In fact, of course, only the hand moves, and that would be hidden behind the pad. Randi, too, later accused Geller of peeking, but asserted that Geller had guessed the number correctly by watching the movement of the pencil top over the notepad, which is just one degree more plausible than the moving-arm theory, but hardly convincing. In any case, neither of the two examples cited above actually amounts to catching Geller in "outright deceptions."

The article goes on to describe how Geller had come to the offices of *Time-Life* to demonstrate his powers and adds that after he left, "Randi . . . duplicated each of his feats, explaining that any magician could perform them." Later, both Randi and Charles Reynolds were to claim that they actually saw Uri bending a fork by pressing it on the tabletop. For some reason, *Time* omits this important piece of "evidence," although it is hard to see why. After all, if they hoped to catch Geller cheating, and Randi actually did catch him, they had every reason to publicize the discovery. The article concludes with the assertion that Geller left Israel in disgrace after a computer expert and some psychologists duplicated his feats and called him a fraud. This statement is factually untrue; Geller left Israel to perform in Germany, then to take part in research at Stanford; there was no disgrace and no exposure.

When Geller returned to America early in 1974, his world triumphs behind him, the onslaught began in earnest. Leading the anti-Geller battalions were the two veterans of the previous campaign, Randi and Charles Reynolds. Randi seized every opportunity to denounce Geller as a fraud, and began preparing a book exposing his "tricks." As the editor of *Popular Photo-*

graphy, Reynolds had reacted with indignation to a report that had appeared on the front page of the British newspaper *The News of the World*, describing how Uri had taken photographs of himself with the lens cap taped over the camera lens. Now this was encroaching on Reynolds' own special field. In the mid-1960s, a Chicago bellhop named Ted Serios had aroused widespread attention by his apparent ability to take "mental photographs." Serios would hold a small cardboard tube over the camera lens, stare into it with intense concentration, and press the button. When developed, the film sometimes revealed images of buildings, vehicles, even people. Reynolds was convinced that Serios achieved his effects by trickery, and in 1967 he and an associate published an article in *Popular Photography* asserting that they had worked out how it was done. According to them, it merely involved palming a color transparency and inserting it into the cardboard tube. As an explanation it was highly plausible—the single objection being that every investigator of Serios had already thought of it, and had therefore examined his cardboard tube before and after the experiments. In spite of this, American magicians continued to refer to Reynolds' "exposure" of Ted Serios.

Now Uri was making the same kind of claim, and Reynolds once again prepared to do battle. A former *Life* photographer, Yale Joel, provided him with the ammunition he needed. Joel spent a day with Uri, and he described it in an article. Uri had taken Joel's Pentax camera, its lens cap taped on tightly, and pressed the camera against his forehead, trying to transmit the picture of an eagle onto the film. Then he suggested that they try a little mind reading, and asked Joel and his assistant to go into the next room and make a drawing. With another camera (the Pentax being in the room with Geller) Joel photographed his assistant making the drawing, which was of a chair. The drawing was put in an envelope, and then into an outer envelope, and taken to Geller. Uri concentrated on the sealed double envelope, seized a pencil, and did an accurate sketch of the chair. After this, he pressed the Pentax against his forehead and tried more psychic photography.

Later, in the developing room, most of the film was found to be blank. But one exposure did contain a blurred image. It showed part of a man's chin and his sweater; most of the picture was covered with a black blot.

Above: the *News of the World* experiments, with Geller trying to photograph himself with a camera that has the lens cap still in position. They used the photographer's own Nikon F.

Right: two rolls of film—which Geller never touched—came out blank. In the middle of the third roll were these two pictures.

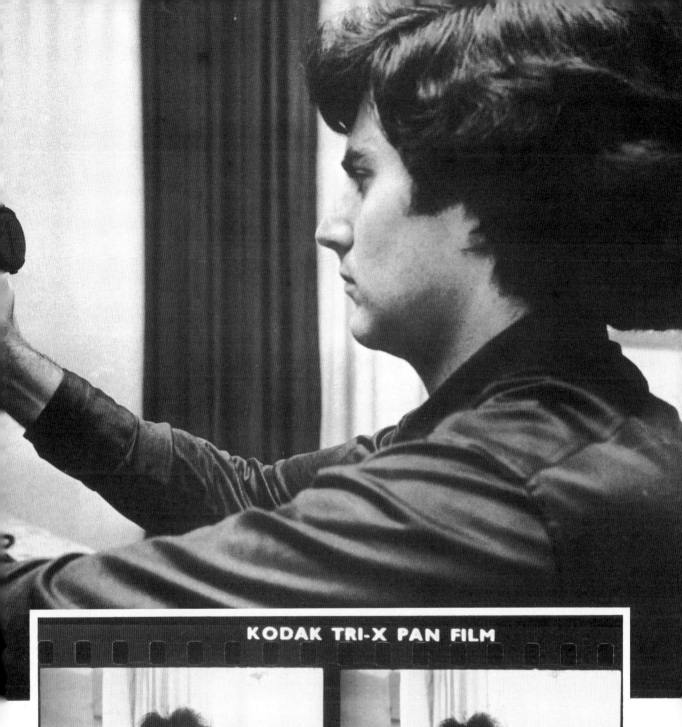

KODAK TRI-X PAN FILM

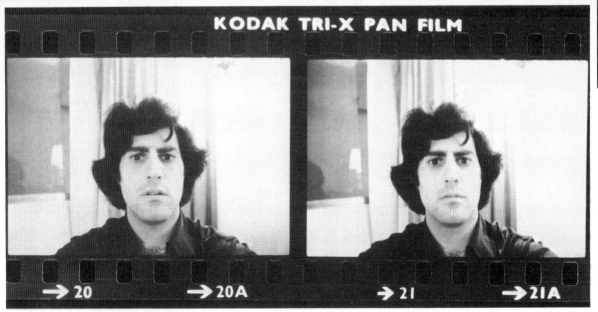

→ 20   → 20A   → 21   → 21A

31

Ted Serios and Uri Geller both attempted to produce mental photographs: but whereas Serios produced views by staring into a camera lens, Geller produced a picture of himself through a lens cap. Right: a Serios "thoughtograph" of Munich's Frauenkirche (far right).

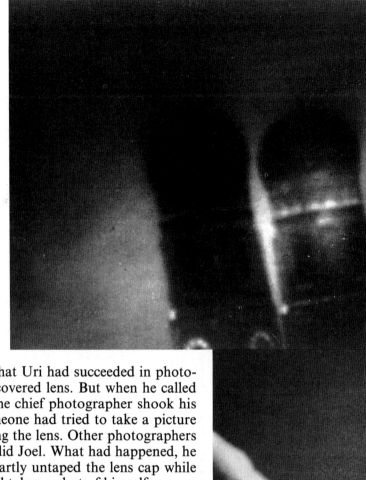

At first, Joel had no doubt that Uri had succeeded in photographing himself through the covered lens. But when he called in at the *Time-Life* Building, the chief photographer shook his head. His verdict was that someone had tried to take a picture with the lens cap *partly* covering the lens. Other photographers agreed. And so, on reflection, did Joel. What had happened, he concluded, was that Uri had partly untaped the lens cap while they were in the next room, and taken a shot of himself.

Joel's photograph, together with an article describing the visit, was published in the June 1974 issue of *Popular Photography*. In the same issue, Charles Reynolds returned to the attack with a long article in which he described the *Time* office episode of the previous year, and asserted that both he and Randi had observed Uri bending a spoon with his hands and bending a latch key by pressing it against a tabletop. He continued with an analysis of the session with Yale Joel, admitting that Geller had succeeded in various mind-reading feats, including "reading" a message in a sealed envelope that had been written by Joel's son before the session. On the "psychic photography," however, it was definitely thumbs down. The article concluded with an outline of Puharich's book on Geller—which is, admittedly, enough to make the most ardent believer shudder with embarrassment.

Reading Joel's article, and looking at the "psychic photograph," the unprejudiced observer has to admit that it looks as if Uri tried cheating. At the same time, there are a few things to be said for the defense. Reynolds was already committed to an anti-Geller position when he (presumably) sent Joel to spend the day with Geller. The *Time* editors, who pointed out the deception, were also anti-Geller; and Joel had been a photographer for *Time-Life*. If Joel was there to observe Geller critically, why didn't he count how many pictures Geller snapped before he and

his assistant left the room, and again when he returned? It is the kind of thing you would expect a good journalist to do as second nature. If he had made a count, he could have stated with total conviction that the "fake" photograph must have been taken while he was out of the room. Why didn't he? And what about the mind reading? Was that genuine, or was Geller peeping through the keyhole as well as untaping the camera lens?

This is the problem that one encounters again and again in connection with Geller. Skeptics can frequently make a fairly convincing case for some particular incident of cheating; but they usually have to admit that half a dozen other matters remain unexplained. In March 1974, *Time* magazine renewed its attack—not merely on Geller, but on the whole psychic scene.

Below: Serios producing a thoughtograph. When about to shoot, Eisenbud writes, Serios went into a state of intense concentration, ending with an explosive burst of energy at the camera.

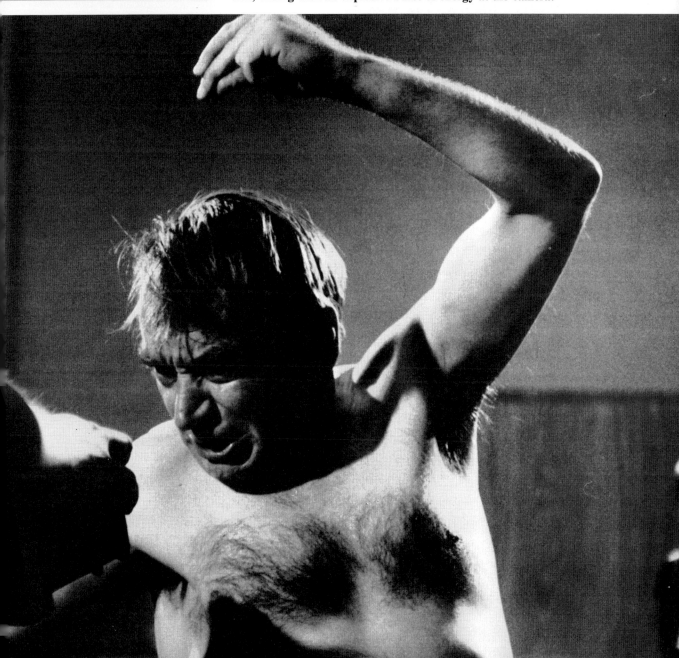

Charles Reynolds was quoted as saying that many agnostics still cling to a belief in black magic, "only now it's called the paranormal." Kirlian photography, ESP research, out-of-the-body experiences, "the secret life of plants," psychic surgery, and Geller's spoon bending were all dismissed as if they were equally preposterous. An insert called "A Long History of Hoaxes" contained one of the famous "fairy" photographs taken by two English girls and published in Conan Doyle's *The Coming of the Fairies*; Ted Serios grimacing at a camera; and some of Professor J. B. Rhine's assistants at the parapsychology laboratory at Duke University. The section includes, inevitably, the story of Charles Reynolds' "exposure" of Ted Serios and seems to imply that Serios was caught cheating.

The weakness of the attack lies in its lack of discrimination. It is possible that psychic surgery is a hoax, that plants cannot really read our minds, that Kirlian photography (photographing the "life-aura" of living creatures) may depend on some simple electrical phenomenon. But to lump all these together as if they were all on the same level of improbability shows a certain lack of discernment. The same applies to the list of "hoaxes." Rhine's careful research into extrasensory perception at Duke University is generally conceded to be serious and sincere, even by people who think his test conditions were too loose. The famous fairy photographs are quite probably a hoax, but no one has ever produced an atom of proof either way, and until someone does, no one can be quite as confident as the editors of *Time* seem to be. And Ted Serios has never at any time been exposed as a fraud—

Above: Geller's "through the lens cap" picture produced with Yale Joel's Pentax. Originally impressed by the picture, Joel came to think Uri had partly untaped the lens cap while Joel was briefly out of the room on another experiment.

Above: a picture of Seth Joel that resembles the Geller photo. Below: but the Seth Joel picture was taken with the lens cap held partly away from the camera, as shown here. They later found that one person could do it alone.

although obviously he might be. We see here a phenomenon that we shall encounter again in relation to Geller: that when a scientist or a "rationalist" sets himself up as the defender of reason, he often treats logic with a disrespect that makes one wonder which side he is on.

In contrast to the other parts of the *Time* article, the attack on Geller is oddly restrained. It does, however, repeat the assertion that a certain Professor Hyman caught him in some "outright deceptions," without specifying what these were. The writer adds that Geller canceled a British tour "after a group of British magicians made plans to catch him in the act . . . citing mysterious death threats." In *My Story*, Geller explains that he canceled the British tour because there had been assassination attempts on prominent Jews, and he had received death threats from Arab terrorist organizations. Anyone who lived in England at the time can verify that there were several assassination attempts, by both Arab and Israeli terrorists, and that Geller's fears were not entirely imaginary.

But by far the strangest item in this issue of *Time* is the letter from the editor on the contents page. Ralph P. Davidson admits there that his Los Angeles correspondent had submitted his fingertips to Kirlian photography and was interested to see that the developed film showed "blotchy, whorled or spiky 'coronas' that corresponded to his different emotional states." In the week before publication, the alarm clock of editor Leon Jaroff—who was responsible for the article—failed to go off on three occasions, making him late for work. "Even more bizarre was the mysterious force that glitched *Time*'s complex computerized copy-processing system on closing night—on almost the precise moment that our psychic phenomena story was fed into it. Against astronomical odds, both of the machines that print out *Time*'s copy stopped working simultaneously. No sooner were the spirits exorcized and the machines back in operation than the IBM computer in effect swallowed the entire cover story; it developed a flaw in its programing that sent the copy circling endlessly through memory loops from which it could not be retrieved."

And so, once again, it sounds rather as if Geller had somehow managed to have the last word.

Future generations are going to find it difficult to understand the bitterness and violence of some of the attacks on Geller. They may conclude that they are part of the malice and envy of the "antisuccess mechanism." This would be less than fair. The blunt truth is that, whatever his strange powers, Uri is not the ideal ambassador for the psychic world. Both hostile and friendly observers have made the same observation: that the center of Uri's universe is Uri himself. In direct personal contact with people he likes, his chief characteristics are sincerity and enthusiasm. In front of reporters or TV cameras, he moves into a higher gear and produces an impression of flamboyant egotism. Martin Ebon, an editor of books on the occult who is basically pro-Geller, observes wryly: "By contrast [with Puharich] Uri Geller is crudely two-dimensional. His drive and egocentricity are that of a rock star; he thrives on the kind of adulation— preferably perpetual—that usually surrounds amplified guitars and voices. Whatever conversation he has circles like a plane caught in an airport approach pattern, around himself and his feats. . . ."

It is true that in his public persona Uri projects a certain modest charm. The trouble is that his self-absorption tends to overrule this, so that a self-congratulatory tone keeps leaking through. Anyone who knows him recognizes this as an amplified version of his boyishness and sincerity; but the overall impression can be unfortunate. The following piece of dialogue from his second appearance, in 1974, on the Jimmy Young Show (BBC Radio) illustrates the point.

YOUNG: "How do you react, Uri, to the comments of some scientists that your feats of telepathy are probably phoney?"

URI (expansively): "Look, Jimmy, I want to be quite honest with you. I have a press conference tomorrow and I want to have as many things to tell to the press which I don't want to say openly here and now. You know, people tell me, don't say this, don't say that. . . . So let me just say . . .because tomorrow I want to go into very deep detail about it to the press . . . [Jimmy Young interrupts to point out that he is at present reaching about 8,000,000 people.] Well, anyhow, Jimmy, the thing is that with all this controversy going on around me, and all these accusations of silly things . . . I mean, people heard of bugs planted in me and so on. . . . But look Jimmy, this earth is built of two kinds of people, those who believe and those who don't believe, and I'm not going to challenge those who don't believe. I have very little sympathy for them. If you don't believe, it's your own problem. . . ."

Right: Geller with Seth Joel in a mind-reading experiment. If the lens cap photography was slightly suspect during the session with the Joels, Geller's other demonstrations were highly successful.

Right: Geller with his mother and yet another bent spoon, in a picture taken by Yale Joel during the same session. Geller's metal-bending power and mind-reading abilities were not disputed by Joel.

What he actually says is reasonable enough, but the way he says it is at once irritating and embarrassing. The emphasis on press conferences, with its connotation of a politician about to make some important announcement, and on the thousands of people who are now discussing him suggests delusions of grandeur. And his implicit disparagement of the Jimmy Young Show, while a guest on that program, is certainly tactless.

In September 1975, I appeared on the BBC's Monday morning program *Start the Week* along with Uri, and television personalities Richard Baker, Esther Rantzen, and others. I had been invited because I was known to believe that Uri's powers are genuine; everyone else in the studio made it plain they thought he was a fake. As I listened to Uri describing how he had been walking along in New York City, and then had suddenly been "teleported" 36 miles away, to come crashing through a screen in the house of Andrija Puharich in Ossining, New York, I felt considerable sympathy. Uri knew perfectly well they were all thinking "bloody liar." A moment later, Richard Baker asked Uri whether he had not claimed to be an instrument of beings from outer space, "the Nine." Uri replied: "No, you're not quoting from my book. You see, there are so many books written about me." I groaned inwardly and shook my head. As far as I knew at that point the only book about him was Puharich's, although Ebon's symposium was on its way. A few moments later Uri repeated his claim: "You see, there are so many books written about me that everybody misinterprets me. . . . I've been called a fraud, a charlatan, I've been called a messiah from God and all that. . . . Now I do not believe that beings from outer

Top: Geller with Jimmy Young in November 1973, on the BBC radio show that started his remarkable London demonstrations. Above: Jimmy Young with the key that Geller bent on the program.

space are watching me. . . . I do not rule that out either. . . . I don't know."

Once again it struck me that if, as Ebon implies, Uri is his own greatest admirer, he is also his own worst enemy. I don't doubt that he was doing his best to answer their questions honestly, fully aware of the general atmosphere of skepticism; but what he appeared to be saying was: "Someone as fascinating and many-sided as myself must expect to be misunderstood. Of course, I don't think I'm God but some of my followers do, and I could be wrong. . . ." At this point, I felt an urgent desire to take him aside and whisper in his ear the critic James Agate's remark: "The British instinctively admire any man who has no talent and is modest about it."

A few weeks before this broadcast, I had had the opportunity to meet Uri's most formidable—or at least, most persistent—opponent, "The Amazing Randi." Randi and I, together with the psychologist Dr. Christopher Evans, attended a showing of the film Andrija Puharich made about the Brazilian psychic healer, Arigó. It was his experiences with Arigó that made Puharich vow he would not miss out next time a gifted psychic appeared. The copy of the film belonged to Dr. Ted Bastin, one of the many distinguished scientists who had tested Uri in England and been convinced of his genuineness.

I have to admit that I found the Arigó film disappointing. Eye-witness accounts of Arigó describe him cutting open stomachs with his rusty knife, tearing out a cancer, then healing the cut by pressing the edges together with his fingers—all in a matter of seconds. The commentary on the film described Arigó removing a cancer, yet the growth removed from the patient's scalp was clearly only a sebaceous cyst. He lanced a boil on a patient's back—not a very hazardous undertaking. He also inserted his knife under a patient's eyelid and apparently scraped the eyeball. The eyeball operation was easily the most dangerous-looking of the three shown. Yet on the whole, the 10-minute film was rather less impressive than Puharich's account of Arigó's operations in his book Uri. Christopher Evans, who had written his doctoral thesis on the eyeball, was not slow to point out that the eyes have no nerves and can be subjected to a remarkable amount of rough treatment without obvious damage. And Randi observed that the patient with the boil had winced as Arigó lanced it, although all accounts of Arigó's operations claim that they were painless.

One of the first things that struck me about Randi was a certain resemblance to Uri—not in appearance but in personality. Both are self-evidently "nice" men, and both have considerable charm. Both are showmen who find it difficult to separate the public and private selves. Every now and then, as you listen to Randi's amusing patter, you become aware that you are an audience rather than an individual. You find yourself glancing over your shoulder to see if, without your noticing, a crowd has gathered.

At dinner, after the Arigó film, Randi caused a number of spoons to bend, and made a watch go forward several hours by rubbing its face. He declined to attempt any mind-reading feats there and then, but invited myself and Dr. Evans to go and see a television film in which he duplicated Geller's act.

I found Randi likable and plausible; the only thing that

Above: George Porter was one of the listeners to the Jimmy Young Show that November day. He was eating his lunch, and rubbed his dessert spoon experimentally. Several other objects, shown here on the table, bent in sympathy.

Below: housewife Dora Portman didn't even need to rub her ladle. As she listened to Geller on the radio, it bent all by itself.

Left: the author with Dr. Christopher Evans, who takes a skeptical attitude about Geller's powers. Clearly, Geller takes people different ways—it appears to be generally agreed that he is a superb showman. The difference of opinion lies in whether or not he is really anything more.

Left: the Amazing Randi, one of Geller's principal detractors, midway in his stage magic act.

bothered me was the sweeping and intense nature of his skepticism. He was obviously working from the premise that all paranormal phenomena, without exception, are fakes or delusions. He seemed to take it for granted that all of us—there were also two women present—shared his opinions, and he made jovial, disparaging remarks about psychics and other such weirdos. I began to get the uncomfortable feeling of a Jew who has accidentally walked into a Nazi meeting, or a Jehovah's Witness at a convention of militant atheists. As a supposedly scientific investigator, Randi struck me as being oddly fixed in his opinions.

The following day, I saw his television film and found it impressive. To begin, Randi performed Houdini's hair-raising trick of escaping from a milk churn filled to the top with water. Then he did some spoon and nail bending, as Geller had done on the same TV show the previous week. The presenter, Alan Spraggett, seemed to be a Geller enthusiast, and kept challenging Randi to duplicate Geller's mind-reading act. Randi acted shy, as if trying to evade the challenge. Finally, Spraggett cornered Randi, and sighing reluctantly, Randi agreed to try. It was a masterly piece of acting. Spraggett then produced an envelope containing a drawing he had made in the utmost secrecy at home. Randi took it for a moment and held it flat between his palms, then handed it back and asked Spraggett to hold it. Meanwhile, he took a sheet of paper and a pen and did a drawing in full view of the camera—a boat with a curlicue of smoke rising from its funnel. He asked Spraggett to open his envelope. Spraggett held up a drawing identical to the one Randi had just done.

As Christopher Evans and I left, we both agreed that it had been an amazing demonstration. There was only one drawback: it was on film, not "for real." This left the obvious possibility that the mind-reading trick was simple collusion between Randi and Spraggett, rather than Randi working by himself. In Randi's book on Geller, he speaks of the TV host Mike Douglas, on whose show both he and Geller have appeared, and remarks that Mike "has played straight man for my magic tricks, and even worked as a confederate a few times."

Randi persisted in asking Spraggett whether, if he (Randi) could duplicate all Geller's tricks, Spraggett would accept him as a messiah with magical powers. Predictably, Spraggett replied no, because Randi admitted that his tricks were straightforward conjuring. This raises the interesting question whether Randi could, if he wanted, set himself up as a psychic, and duplicate all Geller's feats—not only on stage, but also in the laboratory.

During my evening with Randi, he performed only one trick that might have struck me as genuinely magical, in the sense that I could think of no possible method of doing it. He handed me a new pack of cards, and told me to shuffle them. I did this thoroughly. He then told me to separate the cards into two piles in any order I liked, and that, when I had finished, one pile would consist entirely of black cards, one entirely of red. I did as he asked, going through the pack and putting the cards into two random heaps, sometimes putting as many as five cards into one heap before I moved back to the other. There was one slight change of plan; when I had half finished, Randi told me to stop

Above: one of the posters that advertise Randi's performances. As a "genuine" magician, Randi particularly resents Geller's claims to supernormal powers, claiming that his effects can be produced by strictly natural means.

Above: like Houdini, Randi has made some spectacular escapes. In these two pictures, he is shown being locked into a maximum security bank vault, and—less than four minutes later—getting out.

Left: in a demonstration of his physical control, Randi is locked in a sealed coffin, which remains underwater for nearly two hours.

and said that from now on, I would be putting black cards on the red pile and vice versa. When I had finished, Randi turned both piles face upward with a single movement. Just as he said, one pile was entirely black up to the halfway point, then red; the other was entirely red to the halfway point, then black.

If Randi had told me he did *that* trick by supernatural means, I might have believed him. On the other hand, I doubt whether any messiah is going to gain hordes of converts with card tricks.

During dinner that evening, we discussed Randi's forthcoming book on Uri. I expressed my view, for what it was worth, that Uri possessed genuine psychic powers, although I was perfectly willing to admit that some of his effects could be mere conjuring. Randi assured me that when I read his book, I would no longer have the slightest doubt that Geller was a fraud. There were two points on which he laid special insistence. One was that in Israel Geller had actually been a straightforward stage magician—a rabbit-in-the-hat conjurer—before he decided to set up as a psychic. The second was that Uri had been caught cheating in Israel, and had actually been forced to leave in disgrace. The scandal had been so great, said Randi, that Uri had fled to Europe.

A few months later, Ballantine Books in New York published *The Magic of Uri Geller* by James Randi. It must rank as one of the unkindest books written by one celebrity about another. It is a first-rate piece of argumentative writing; almost anyone who reads it from cover to cover will end up absolutely convinced that Geller is a fake. Yet the reason for its success is not that Randi produces a mass of startling and revelatory facts. It is

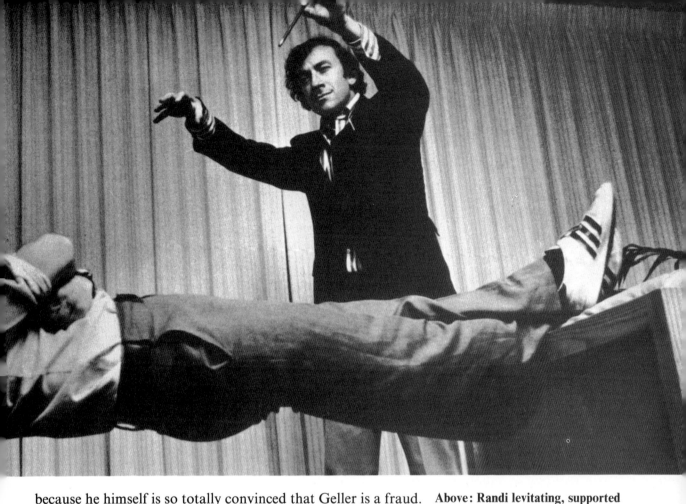

Above: Randi levitating, supported only by his head and heels, as part of his stage magic show.

because he himself is so totally convinced that Geller is a fraud. He says it with such sturdy conviction, over and over again, that it ultimately has a kind of hypnotic effect. The 18th-century agnostic Tom Paine argued against miracles by asking whether it is more likely that a man should tell a lie or that nature should disobey her own laws. Randi keeps asking, in effect, whether it is more likely that Uri should be a clever trickster, or a miracle worker who derives his powers from some extraterrestrial source. And because his fundamental belief is that there is no such thing as the paranormal, there can be only one possible answer. After a dozen or so pages of this, the fair-minded reader asks himself: "Could Randi be right?" And then he has to admit that according to Randi's premises he must be right.

Occasionally, however, a reader's initial acceptance of Randi's argument may give way to doubts. In my own case, the doubts began to appear after Randi had me more than half convinced. A man who rejects Geller's paranormal claims on the grounds of pure logic owes it to his reader to play the game according to his own rules. This Randi often fails to do. In the chapter on *Time*'s handling of the Geller case, he quotes Puharich: "We [Uri and Puharich] also found out that the 'Time' correspondent in Jerusalem had filed a report on Uri that said that scientists from Hebrew University claimed they had caught him cheating. This, too, proved to be a lie. . . ." But it *isn't* a lie, says Randi; has Puharich never seen the Jerusalem *Post* article headed "Tele-pathist Geller Termed a Fraud" of October 5, 1970? The *Post* story, which Randi goes on to relate, tells how a computer expert, Yosef Allon, had been impressed by Uri's act until Uri performed a card trick that Allon had been doing for years. His suspicions aroused, Allon and three Hebrew University colleagues settled down to working out how Uri did his other tricks. "Last week," the *Post* article continues, "they demonstrated the results by performing a series of Geller's acts before an impressed audience of the University's psychology department. The four then explained that the feats of 'thought transference' were accomplished mainly by sleight of hand. . . ."

In fact, Puharich was right, and *Time* and Randi are wrong. *Time* claimed that scientists had caught Geller cheating, but they had done nothing of the sort. They had *assumed* he was cheating, then duplicated his tricks in front of an audience, which is not the same thing at all. Moreover, the wording of the Jerusalem *Post* extract seems to suggest that the tricks they duplicated were only those involving thought transference—not key bending, watch repairing, and other Geller feats. Were these, too, alleged to be fraudulent? The headline itself says Geller has been "termed" a fraud, not proved a fraud. It is the Charles Reynolds-Ted Serios story all over again. Of course, Geller may have been cheating; he admits to some cheating in Israel, at the insistence of his manager, as we have already seen. But no one "proved" it.

The chapter entitled "He Didn't Fool Them in Israel" ought to be one of the most devastating in Randi's book, and at a casual glance it appears to be just that. The chapter heading reads: "At home, Geller comes a cropper with the law and the press when students are able to outperform him; charged in court, he is found guilty of breach of contract; Israel deduces there is nothing paranormal about his performances—it's only tricks."

What Randi appears to be asserting is that Geller was caught cheating, landed in trouble with the law, and was taken to court. When you read the heading more closely, of course, you see that the court case was nothing to do with "coming a cropper with the law." But if you then read the chapter itself, to elicit more details, you will find no mention of either an encounter with the law or the court case for breach of contract (Uri claimed that his manager had been cheating him). The chapter is devoted entirely to quoting at length from an article in "the well-known Israeli weekly *Haolam Hazeh*" denouncing Geller as a fraud. The core of this article is an admission by Hannah Shtrang, sister of Uri's close friend and bodyguard Shipi, that Uri and Shipi were confederates, and that they worked their tricks through secret signals. She herself, she says, occasionally took part.

If true, this is certainly very damaging indeed. But even on purely logical grounds it is hard to take seriously. In *My Story*, Uri hints that there was an affair between himself and Hannah. Hannah is quoted as saying that a romance started between them, and that it has continued up to the present time. She maintains that Uri's other girlfriends "have been mere decoys" and that "he always returns to me." She goes on to say that Uri has very special supernatural powers, but also uses trickery.

Haolam Hazeh is an Israeli magazine that specializes in sensational stories about well-known personalities; to call it "the well-known Israeli weekly" suggests a respectability to which it

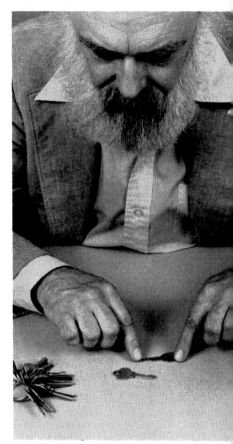

Above: Randi's version of Geller's key bending. He claims this method is perfectly possible for anyone of normal strength to master. The first step is to select the key carefully. Brass and aluminum are more easily bent than steel. At least one key must have a slot in the head, instead of a round hole. Having selected two keys, show the audience that they are flat.

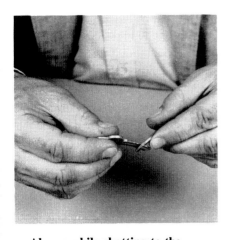

Above: while chatting to the audience and establishing eye-to-eye contact, hide with one hand the action of hooking the end of one key through the slot in the other. The slot serves as a fulcrum for gaining leverage to bend the key. The operation is shown unconcealed for clarity. As in many magic tricks, the key is bent before the action begins. Top right: then place the keys in the volunteer's hand and curl his fingers quickly over the keys.

Above right: hold your fist over the volunteer's hand holding the keys and concentrate intensely or intone impressively, "Bend, bend."

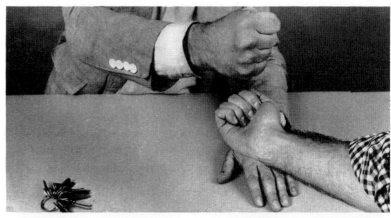

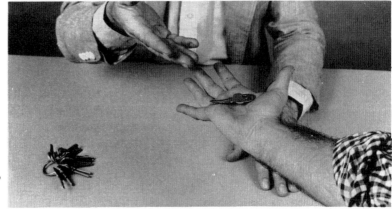

Right: to the audience's amazement, when the volunteer's hand opens, one of the keys has indeed bent.

Right: exhibiting the bent key.

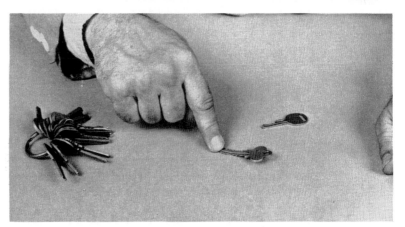

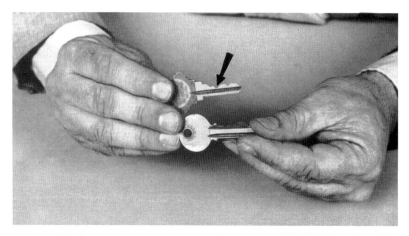

Left: another method, using only a single key, is best done with a key with a deep cut near the center, like the key at the top.

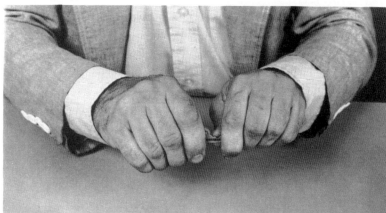

Left: making a momentary turn away from the audience—looking for "better light," for example—apply heavy pressure with the thumbs to produce a bent key.

could never lay claim. This leads us to wonder why Hannah, who remains a close friend of Uri's, and whose brother remains his traveling companion, should spill the beans to such a magazine. The logical inference is that she did not, or that what she actually said was considerably distorted.

The *Haolam Hazeh* article does describe the promised episode of the Israeli students who "outperformed" Geller, but they turn out to be the same four Hebrew University scientists we have already encountered, who merely duplicated some of his mind-reading feats. The magazine story says they spoiled a TV show by shouting from the audience; it is not clear how this qualifies as "outperforming him." Nor did Uri's legal troubles result from this event.

The final verdict on Randi's book has to be that it fails for the same reason as the March 1973 *Time* article: because it is too obviously biased. Physicists Russell Targ and Hal Puthoff have gone to the trouble of issuing an eight-page report correcting downright misstatements (24 in all) in the 12-page chapter on their experiments at Stanford. (For example, Randi asserts that Shipi Shtrang was present at the Stanford experiments; he was not.) It *could* have been a brilliant and devastating book, if Randi had taken the trouble to give the Devil his due, and to sound balanced and unprejudiced. As it is, his tone will irritate the very people he is most anxious to convince: the reasonable, open-minded people who want to be presented with the facts, and then allowed to judge for themselves. This is a pity; for I am willing to give Randi credit for being as sincere as Uri Geller.

The Geller method, by Geller.
Top: Uri rubs the key with his
finger as it lies flat on the table.
Above: Geller stroking the key
he has placed in the bowl of a
spoon. He claims that the other
metal strengthens his power.
Left: Geller stroking the key
on its side. On many occasions
keys have bent, and his supporters
point out that while Geller bends
these keys there is no opportunity
for sleight-of-hand operations
as demonstrated by James Randi.

47

3

The Scientists Investigate

Uri Geller, with his seemingly inexhaustible ability to read the minds and bend the cutlery of the world, offers scientists the hope of a repeatable psychic experiment, and as a result he has spent days in laboratories with scientists all over the world. Right: a Kirlian photo of Geller's finger sending a burst of energy during one of his demonstrations. Below: Geller's finger at rest.

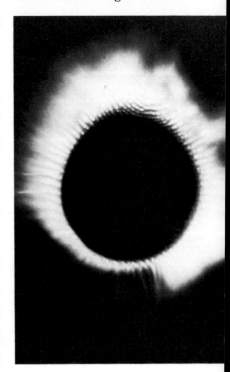

For more than 100 years now, scientists have been inviting psychics and mediums into their laboratories to submit their powers to careful testing. And it must be admitted that the results have been, on the whole, rather disappointing. It is not that the psychics have failed to produce the results. On the contrary, some of the phenomena have been spectacular: accordions played by invisible hands, tables rising off the floor in broad daylight, flowers appearing out of the air—one medium apparently materialized a six-foot golden lily, complete with plant pot. But the basic rule for a scientific experiment is that it should be *repeatable*. And the basic

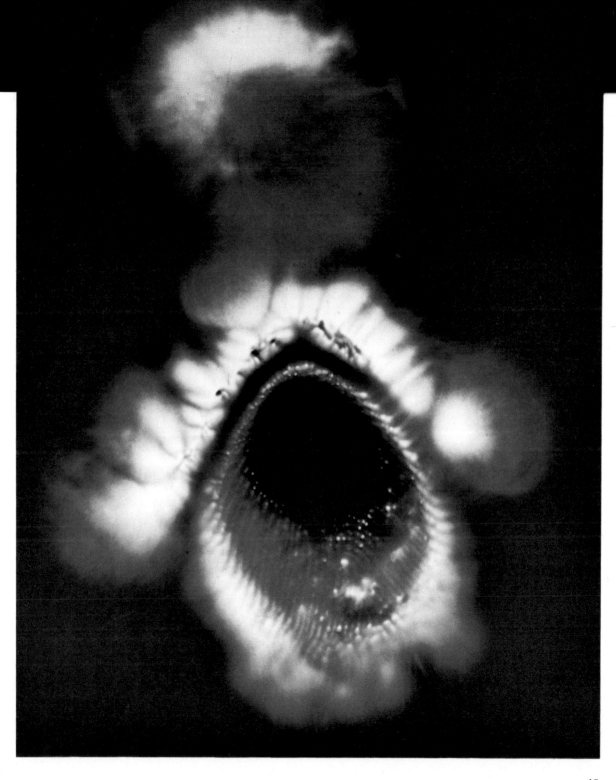

"It is difficult to think of an experiment that would be harder to fake"

trouble with psychical phenomena is that they seem to be as temperamental as opera singers; they perform seemingly according to whim, and cannot be pinned down to a schedule. Again and again, individual investigators have "proved" the reality of telepathy, psychokinesis, second sight, and the power to foretell the future. And still nobody is absolutely convinced—least of all, the scientists themselves.

This is why psychical researchers rub their hands with delight whenever a really gifted psychic appears—someone who seems able to call upon his powers at will. In the whole history of psychical research, there have been fewer than a dozen such people. As soon as Puharich heard reports of Uri Geller's powers, he realized that this could be the breakthrough everyone had been seeking. Of course, it was just as likely that Geller was simply a clever trickster—more likely, in fact, because there are more con men in the world than miracle workers. Therefore, his first task was to check Geller—to the best of his own ability—and then to get him into a well-equipped laboratory.

As we have seen, it took Puharich only one hour to decide that Geller's telepathy was genuine. Some of the "debunkers" have used this as evidence that Puharich was credulous and overtrustful. But it is difficult to see how this charge can be sustained. Geller wrote something on a pad, placed it face downward on a table, then told Puharich to think of three numbers. When Puharich picked up the pad, his three numbers had *already* been written on it. Few experiments would be harder to fake.

The same applies to Puharich's thermometer experiment, conducted the following day. It may sound easy enough for a stage magician to raise the temperature of a thermometer by trickery, particularly if he is allowed to handle it or breathe on it. But it is difficult to see how this could be done if the thermometer was on the other side of the room, as Puharich alleges.

Puharich's next move was to speak to astronaut Ed Mitchell, the sixth man to land on the moon. On his 1971 moon flight Mitchell performed an experiment in telepathy, attempting to transmit a series of numbers to four friends on earth. The result was astonishing: not because the number of hits was high, but because it was incredibly low—far below what would have been expected by chance. You might compare this result to someone who overhears a conversation in a foreign language of which he knows a few words, and gets a completely mistaken impression of what it is all about. But he could get such a mistaken impression only if he partly understood the language. Ed Mitchell's friends obviously "overheard" something, which they proceeded to get all wrong. This was intriguing enough to make Mitchell decide to persist in his investigations into the paranormal. When he left the army, he set up an Institute of Noetic Sciences—that is, studies relating to the intellect. Its aim was to try to investigate the ways in which people can use their psychic energies.

Geller arrived in the United States for the first time in August 1972; he stayed at Puharich's house in Ossining, New York. Ed Mitchell came, together with Dr. Gerald Feinberg of the Physics Department of Columbia University, and a number of other scientists. Uri demonstrated his powers; he caused the hands of a watch to move, and broke a steel ring and a sewing

Above: Geller with the former astronaut Ed Mitchell. The two met early in Geller's first trip to the United States in 1972, and Mitchell was instrumental in getting Uri tested by scientists.

Left: Mitchell on the moon. While on the moon flight, Mitchell tried some unauthorized experiments with telepathy, trying to transmit a series of numbers to friends on earth. The results intrigued him enough to involve him full time in a study of psychic energies after he resigned from the space program.

needle. Both Mitchell and Feinberg were convinced. Mitchell was so impressed that he offered to put up the cash to pay for further investigation of Uri's powers at the Stanford Research Institute, at Menlo Park, California—an independent organization, not connected with Stanford University.

Mitchell was eager to get the opinion of his friend Wernher von Braun, the famous rocket scientist, who is a vice-president of a large industrial corporation in Germantown, Maryland. Von Braun's attitude, like that of most scientists, was distinctly skeptical, but Geller's demonstrations soon had him convinced. Von Braun held his wedding ring in his own hand, without allowing Geller to touch it. Geller held his own hand near von Braun's—without touching it; the ring slowly bent into an oval shape. Later, as Geller and Puharich were about to leave, von Braun discovered that his pocket electronic calculator was not operating, although it had a new battery. Uri took it in his hands for a moment and concentrated. The battery then began to work, but the calculator itself seemed to have gone haywire. After another 30 seconds of hard concentrating, Uri succeeded in making it operate normally. Understandably, von Braun was convinced that Geller's powers were genuine.

During all this time, according to his book *Uri*, Puharich was still in contact with his "extraterrestrial intelligences." Two days before the von Braun demonstration, the tape recorder held a conversation with Puharich, in Uri's presence, in which it explained that the Space Beings were planning to land on the earth within the next year or two—they declined to specify exactly when—and told Puharich to write a comprehensive book on "the UFO experience." They also explained that a sudden petulant outburst from Uri the day before, on the subject of a documentary film script, had been inspired by them. Shortly after this, the tape recorder again talked to Puharich, explaining that he would soon be "on his own," and implying that they

Left: a photo Uri Geller took out of the window of a jet traveling between England and Germany. Uri took the picture when his camera levitated in front of him— at that time he could not see anything in the sky. It was only when the film was developed that these images of UFOs flying alongside the jet appeared.

Left: sketches by BOAC pilot Captain J. R. Howard in 1954 of a formation of UFOs that flew parallel to his Stratocruiser for more than 80 miles on a trans-atlantic flight. The sketches formed part of his voyage report. He said that there were six small black objects and a larger "flying jellyfish" that appeared to change shape constantly. Many of the 51 passengers aboard later admitted they had also seen the formation in the sky on the flight. Uri's experience of seeing UFOs from a plane was not the first.

would shortly cease to communicate. A few days later, the same voice told Puharich that Uri was not to go to California for the Stanford research. Understandably, Puharich was bewildered and furious, and decided to ignore the voice. Uri himself became furious when Puharich told him that, whatever happened, the Stanford project had to go ahead, and he threw a sugar bowl at Puharich. Puharich, in his own words, "cursed the gods," which apparently provoked an instant storm that rocked the house. During the storm a grandfather clock in the hall shot across the floor and virtually exploded.

This preposterous incident may seem to have no place in an account of the laboratory investigations of Uri's powers. In fact, it could well offer a vital clue. To begin with, the disembodied voice sounds highly knowledgeable about science and mathematics, although most of its communications seem to be sheer gobbledegook. For example:

THE VOICE: "Don't you see an ashtray and a key appeared right now?"

PUHARICH: "Yes, I did."

THE VOICE: "To your own timeless situation, that means to you there is time. It looks like it happened right now, spontaneously, immediately, straightforward. But that is wrong. For us, that was planned hundreds, hundreds of light-years ago, Andrija...."

Now, as anyone with even the most amateurish interest in astronomy knows, a light-year is not a measurement of time; it is the amount of *space* a beam of light could travel in a year. Interestingly, this is a mistake that Uri himself tends to make.

Again, the English of the voice is oddly colloquial and ungrammatical: "right now," "spontaneously, immediately, straightforward," as they are used in that fragment, suggest Uri's own idiosyncratic English. And the comment "To your own timeless situation, that means to you there is time" also sounds curiously like Uri.

Right: Geller with John Lennon, of Beatles fame, talking about their mutual interest in UFOs.

Above: Russell Targ, a laser physicist with a continuing interest in psychic phenomena. He joined the Stanford Research Institute (which does research on a vast range of subjects, both military and commercial) in 1972, when the Geller tests began there.

Below: Dr. Hal Puthoff, also a laser physicist, who came to SRI in 1971, primarily to do psychic research. He holds various patents on laser and other optical devices.

Finally, there is the extraordinary nature of the communication itself: the suggestion that the whole Stanford project should be dropped. If the Space Beings really were eager to establish Uri as a messenger, they would surely *want* him to be tested by scientists. This sudden objection is a little too abrupt to make sense.

Yet we know, from what Puharich says, that Uri was doubtful about the scientific experiments from the beginning. Ed Mitchell noticed the same thing about him. And Uri's reaction when Puharich said they ought to go ahead anyway—hurling a sugar bowl at him—was uncharacteristically violent.

The obvious conclusion would seem to be that Uri planted the messages on the tape recorder, taking advantage of Puharich's belief in beings from outer space. But if that is so, how did the tape recorder reply to Puharich's questions? For it seems clear from Puharich's book that the conversation was reasonably spontaneous. And how did Uri raise a storm and cause a grandfather clock to smash?

This last question is one that must be explored at length later on. All that need be said here is that if the freak storm and the smashing of the clock were not due to natural causes, they may have been engineered by Uri himself—perhaps unconsciously. In the field of psychical research, such manifestations are lumped together under the term "poltergeist activity." The word *poltergeist*, meaning "noisy ghost," covers a multitude of peculiar phenomena, seemingly caused by some mischievous spirit. It will throw things, move heavy objects, even cause fires. Most parapsychologists now agree that a poltergeist is not a real ghost, but some kind of unconscious manifestation of a living person, usually a disturbed child or adolescent. The person at the center of the disturbance is seldom consciously aware that he or she is responsible.

Puharich's book makes it clear that all kinds of poltergeist activities took place in Uri's presence; objects would fall from the air or suddenly "dematerialize" and appear in another place. So when we learn that Geller was extremely reluctant to go to Stanford, it becomes clear why the voice suddenly ordered Puharich to cancel the trip—and why Uri was so furious when Puharich declined.

As it happened, Uri's apprehension was groundless. During the next few months, he took part in two series of experiments at Stanford, under the supervision of two physicists, Hal Puthoff and Russell Targ. The results seemed to prove conclusively that whatever the nature of Geller's powers, they were undoubtedly genuine.

What Puthoff and Targ thought about Uri is another matter. The first thing he told them, when they met at San Francisco Airport on November 11, 1972, was that his powers came from beings in outer space. Puharich was shocked and alarmed, because the voice had sworn them both to silence. Later, as they sat around a table, Uri asked for silence, explaining that he was waiting for a sign. The bell of an automatic test machine suddenly rang, although there was no reason for it to do so. A copper ring was compressed into the shape of a dumbbell, and then apparently fell through the table and onto the floor underneath. This con-

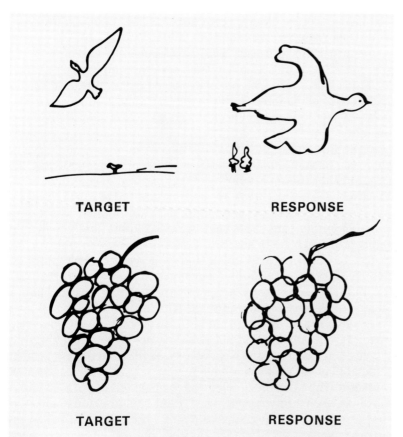

TARGET   RESPONSE

TARGET   RESPONSE

Above: Geller during one of the SRI tests. The envelope he holds contains the target drawing. Left: two of the most successful from the second series of SRI information transmission tests. For this series Geller was shielded from the experimenter making the drawing, in a special room in which he was wholly isolated. Only after Geller was in this room was the target chosen and drawn. Note that Geller duplicated exactly the right number of grapes.

vinced Puharich that the Space Beings had no objection to Uri's revelations about them. Uri asked for one more sign. He asked to look at a chain-bracelet worn by Hal Puthoff, then asked Puthoff to hold it in his own hand. He concentrated for a moment; when Puthoff looked at the bracelet again, it was broken, and one link was missing.

On Monday November 13, the series of laboratory experiments began. First of all, Targ and Puthoff tried an experiment with which another psychic, Ingo Swann, had been successful a few months earlier. A magnetometer—specifically a Bell gauss-meter—was protected by a superconducting shield, and Uri then attempted to deflect the needle by moving his hands near it. The shield's function was to eliminate the possibility of Uri moving the needle by concealing magnets in his sleeve. As Geller concentrated, there was a clear deflection of the needle. The effort obviously exhausted him.

The next day's work was altogether less successful from the scientific point of view, but included some interesting effects. Uri concentrated on trying to bend a brass ring out of shape. Meanwhile he was being filmed, and an x-ray of his hand was visible on a television monitor. When he concentrated, there was a distortion of the picture on the monitor. Moreover, a computer on the floor below began to go wrong, and continued to malfunction as long as Uri was being tested. On the other hand, the brass ring showed only a slight change of shape. When Ed Mitchell, who was present, later reported on this first series of experiments, he omitted all mention of this one, suggesting that neither he nor the others were convinced by the metal bending, or at least regarded it as scientifically unproved.

Tests in ESP, however, were spectacularly successful. A die was placed in a closed box, which was then vigorously shaken by Targ or Puthoff. The box was placed on a table, and Geller had to call out which side of the die he thought uppermost. The box was then opened to check his guess. Geller scored eight out of eight.

Eight aluminum film cans were placed in a row, and an assistant placed some small object inside one of them, choosing the container at random. Then Geller was allowed to enter the room, together with the scientists. He was not allowed to touch the cans, but had to guess which were empty. As he pointed to the presumably empty cans these were removed, until finally he would indicate the can he believed to contain the hidden object. The experiment was tried 14 times, and Geller was correct 12 times. On the other two occasions, he declined to answer; in these trials the hidden objects were a paper-wrapped ball bearing and a sugar cube. In the successful experiments, the hidden objects were unwrapped ball bearings, magnets, and cups containing water. (Geller claims that his power comes from metal and that it is easier for him to bend a spoon or fork if he can place it against a metal plate or radiator.)

In another experiment, a laboratory balance was placed under a bell jar, with a tiny weight—one gram—on one of its pans. Uri then concentrated on trying to depress the empty pan. The recording needle of the balance showed that some force had been applied to the empty pan—many times greater than could have been caused naturally by rocking the table or vibrating the bell jar.

But the experiments that impressed the scientists most were those demonstrating Uri's feats of mind reading. Some drawings had been made on cards before Uri arrived at Stanford. The

Left: Geller with Targ, who looks on as Uri draws the face of the die concealed in the metal box.

scientists did not see the drawings—which were done by assistants—so it would be impossible for Uri to learn anything from them. The cards were sealed in double envelopes. Immediately before the experiment, the scientists would take an envelope from the safe, open it, then take the drawing into the next room, where Uri was waiting. The drawings Uri made were almost exact reproductions of the "target" pictures.

The question that intrigued Targ and Puthoff was how far Geller was using telepathy (mind-to-mind communication), as opposed to clairvoyance (extrasensory perception of objects or events). Obviously, telepathy was out of the question in the die experiments, because nobody knew which way the die had fallen. But a drawing, though in itself an object, has been done by a person, who conceivably could transmit it telepathically to the subject. In the second series of tests, conducted a few weeks later, the scientists deliberately made conditions more difficult. After Geller had successfully reproduced a number of drawings under the same conditions as before, the experimenters devised a method that would almost eliminate the possibility of telepathy. One hundred drawings were made by various people in the building and placed in sealed envelopes. Twenty of these were selected at random, and Geller was asked to try to draw them, one after the other. This time he failed, saying that the pool of 100 target drawings was too large and confusing. On each of three days he made a dozen drawings that he felt to be associated with the pool; only two out of the 12 looked at all like any of the day's 20 targets. He achieved moderate success only on the third day, when two of his drawings were close replicas of two of that day's targets. All this seems to suggest that, where the duplication of drawings is concerned, Geller relies on mind reading.

On the other hand, when drawings were made on the face of a cathode ray tube, or stored in a computer's memory, Geller's response was more accurate. This does not prove, of course, that he could read a computer's memory; but it suggests that he could read the minds of the scientists involved.

Two years later, on October 18, 1974, the results of this second set of experiments were finally published in *Nature*, the highly regarded scientific journal. Targ and Puthoff were determined to bring their research to the attention of the scientific community. The newspaper publicity that followed publication had a distinctly negative tone—the anti-Geller reaction had been

gaining force since his English triumph in 1973. The skeptics pointed out that Targ and Puthoff were significantly silent about Geller's metal-bending activities. Few of them acknowledged the truly remarkable nature of the evidence for ESP, particularly telepathy. And as usual, the magicians alleged that the whole thing had been done by trickery.

Yet, by the time the *Nature* report appeared, a number of English scientists had become totally convinced of the reality of Geller's powers and had no hesitation about publishing their findings.

Ever since he had appeared on the Dimbleby TV program with Geller, Professor John Taylor of London University had been eager to test Uri in his laboratory. The first tests were conducted on February 2, 1974. Taylor knew enough about the Stanford research to know that Puthoff and Targ had been unable to validate Geller's ability to bend metal. This was not because they had not tried. The trouble was that Uri could bend spoons only by stroking them with his finger, and Puthoff and Targ realized that this was far from scientifically foolproof. Taylor decided that this problem could be overcome. Among the objects he gathered for testing was an aluminum strip sealed into a glass tube—by melting the glass—so that there was no way of getting at the metal without breaking the tube. He also worked out a simple device that would actually measure the pressure Uri was applying to anything he stroked. Some pieces of metal were also sealed into tubes made of wire mesh—perhaps in deference to Geller's belief that metal increases his power. Of course, a wire mesh tube can be bent by hand; but in that case it would show the marks of manual pressure.

The first test was a failure; Geller tried to bend a strip of metal without touching it, and failed completely. Another strip of metal lying on a nearby tray was found to be bent after the experiment; but that, of course, could hardly be admitted as evidence, because Geller could have bent it when he was not being observed.

Next, Taylor held a spoon by its bowl, while Geller stroked the stem. After only a few seconds, the thin part of the stem seemed to become soft; then it broke in two. The metal seemed to harden instantly. Taylor had been able to observe throughout

TARGET · RESPONSE 1 · RESPONSE 2 · RESPONSE 3

TARGET · RESPONSE

TARGET · RESPONSE

TARGET · RESPONSE

that almost no pressure was being applied to the spoon by Uri.

After two or three more inconclusive experiments, it was observed that one of the strips of metal in a wire mesh tube had been bent. The tube itself showed no sign of having been tampered with, and Taylor was convinced that Geller would have had no opportunity anyway.

The most impressive experiment in that session was with a Geiger counter, a device for measuring atomic radiation. By intense concentration, holding it in his hands, Uri succeeded in deflecting the needle. The characteristic "chatter" of the Geiger counter, amplified by a loudspeaker, rose to a kind of wail, suggesting the presence of dangerous radioactive material. As soon as Uri relaxed, the wail stopped. He did this three times, on one occasion causing the "chatter" to rise to a high-pitched scream as a machine registered 1000 counts per second. The background radiation of an ordinary room is about two counts per second.

In a second series of experiments, in June 1974, Taylor measured exactly how much pressure was applied to a strip of metal to bend it. A brass strip was taped across a fine balance, so that any pressure on the strip was measured on the dial. Geller gently rubbed the strip, the pointer revealing that he never applied more than half an ounce of pressure; nevertheless, the strip was soon bent by 10 degrees. What was rather more astonishing was that

Above: more of the target pictures and Geller's responses during the SRI tests. The results suggested that Geller relies more on mind reading than on perception of the object itself to duplicate the drawings: his results were much better when there was a possibility of mind-to-mind communication.

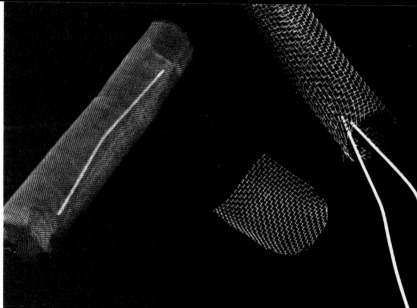

Above: John Taylor, a professor of
mathematics at London University,
who tested Geller in London.

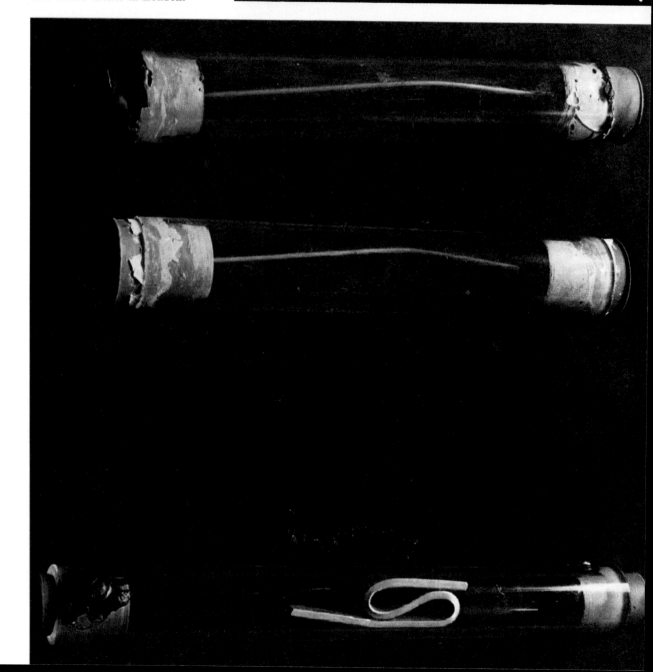

Above: Uri trying to influence a Geiger counter at the Lawrence Radiation Laboratory, Livermore, California, not far from SRI.

Above left: the wire mesh tubes used in John Taylor's experiments to shield some metal bars, which Geller still succeeded in bending.

Left: metal rods encased within sealed plastic tubes, which none-theless were bent by Geller, although he could not touch them.

the pointer itself bent at an angle of 70 degrees, although Geller had not touched this at all.

The *piece de résistance* of Taylor's apparatus was a small metal cylinder that generated an electric current when its end was pressed, measuring the exact degree of pressure. This was embedded in an aluminum strip, and Uri was asked to bend the strip by rubbing it. After a few moments, the strip began to bend; but the especially constructed cylinder suddenly ceased to register. Taylor took it in his hand and peered at it. As he looked, a tiny hole appeared in the center of the sensitive end, and then suddenly the end crumbled away. As Taylor remarked: "The Geller effect had been validated, but at the cost of £200-worth of apparatus." The metal strip continued to bend for the next three minutes.

A crystal inside a plastic container was broken as Geller held his hands over it; Taylor could see the gap between the hands and the container. An aluminum disk inside another plastic container was bent the same way, this time with Taylor holding his hands between Geller's hands and the container.

An attempt to bend a copper strip without touching it was apparently unsuccessful, although the strip was found to be bent some minutes later, when they were engaged in another experiment. And at this point, poltergeist phenomena began to occur. A piece of brass on the other side of the laboratory bent of its own accord, then flew the length of the laboratory, falling near the door. A piece of copper followed it. Then a plastic tube containing an iron rod jumped off a nearby table and struck Taylor's legs; when they examined it, they discovered that the iron rod had been bent so that it touched both sides of the tube.

Finally, Geller influenced a compass, making its needle move by moving his hands over it, a trick that most magicians accomplish by concealing a magnet in the sleeve. But Geller allayed this suspicion by turning the force on and off at will while his hands continued to move over the compass.

It is hardly surprising, then, that John Taylor allowed himself to be totally convinced of Geller's powers. But he was not the first British scientist to be convinced; that distinction should probably go to Cambridge mathematician Dr. Ted Bastin, who traveled to America early in 1973, before the Dimbleby show, to observe Geller in Philadelphia. Bastin had then observed most of the "Geller effects" at first hand—although not under test conditions. But what impressed him most was the disappearance of a plastic box of screwdrivers from a table, and its reappearance in another room, with all the screwdrivers broken. Bastin sent the screwdrivers for testing to a metallurgist colleague, Dr. Chilton, at Cambridge. What he wanted to know, presumably, was whether the fractures had occurred through ordinary bending—for example, by pressing the screwdrivers against a table. Dr. Chilton examined the fractures under a microscope, and had to admit that he was puzzled; they were not of any type he had seen before, and were certainly not due to ordinary bending with fingers and thumbs. There were, in fact, several different types of fracture—including an area that looked as if it had been subjected to intense heat.

On June 21, 1974, soon after the second series of experiments in John Taylor's laboratory, Geller went along to the laboratory of the physics department at Birkbeck College, London, to confront a distinguished gathering that included the writer Arthur Koestler, Professor John Hasted (professor of experimental physics at Birkbeck), Professor David Bohm (theoretical physics), Ted Bastin, Keith Birkinshaw, theoretical physicist Jack Sarfatt, and psychical researcher Brendan O'Regan. At this session Geller repeated feats he had already performed for John Taylor: he bent metal (in this case, door keys), caused a Geiger counter to chatter furiously, and bent an aluminum disk in a plastic container. In this experiment Sarfatt's hand was between Geller's and the container as Geller concentrated.

The following day, those present included Koestler, Arthur C. Clarke (the science fiction writer), A. V. Cleaver (former Rockets director of Rolls Royce), and the pianist Byron Janis. Geller duplicated a drawing made by Koestler, and again influenced the Geiger counter. This time, Koestler had an electrical sensation as Geller influenced the sounds from the Geiger counter.

One of the most impressive experiments, from a scientific point of view, took place with Hasted, Bohm, and Bastin on September 10 of the same year. A number of small objects, including two pieces of vanadium foil from an electron microscope, were sealed in plastic tubes about one centimeter long. One of the scientists covered the various objects loosely with his hand; Geller placed his own hand on top of this. One of the small capsules was seen to leap like a jumping bean. When this capsule was examined, they could see that part of the vanadium foil was missing. Subsequent examination indicated that Geller had dematerialized a part of the foil while it was still sealed in the capsule.

It was also at this session that one of the scientists—the report does not specify which one—took the two halves of a broken spoon from Geller's hand, and discovered that the broken metal was still plastic and soft—a phenomenon that John Taylor had also observed. This seems to suggest that Geller's spoon bending involves some kind of temporary softening of the metal, yet without the heat that would accompany melting. Hostile magicians had frequently suggested that Geller used some kind of chemical to cause the effect. But laboratory examination of the broken metal has proved conclusively on several occasions that no chemical change had taken place in the metal.

All these tests had taken place before the publication of the Stanford report in *Nature* so it might have seemed that Geller—and his defenders—were fighting on fairly secure ground. But in the field of research into the paranormal, things are never as simple as that. To begin with, Professor Taylor had complicated the issue by investigating in his laboratory a number of children who were reportedly able to bend metal by rubbing it. It was a reasonable thing for Taylor to do, because all Geller's demonstrations on radio or TV were followed by dozens of telephone calls from people who claimed that their spoons had bent or that broken watches had started to work. Taylor dismissed the idea that Geller might be indirectly responsible for these effects (assuming that they were genuine). It seemed an altogether more reasonable assumption that he somehow "triggered" the power in other people, giving them confidence that they could do it too.

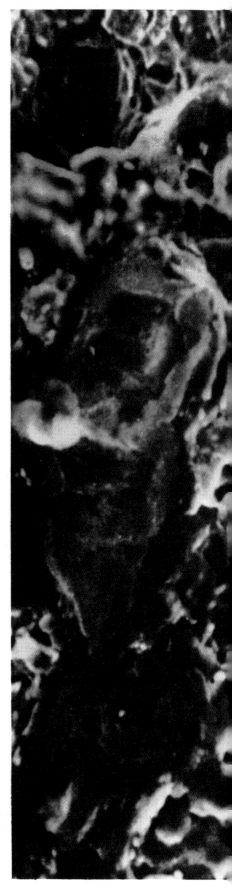

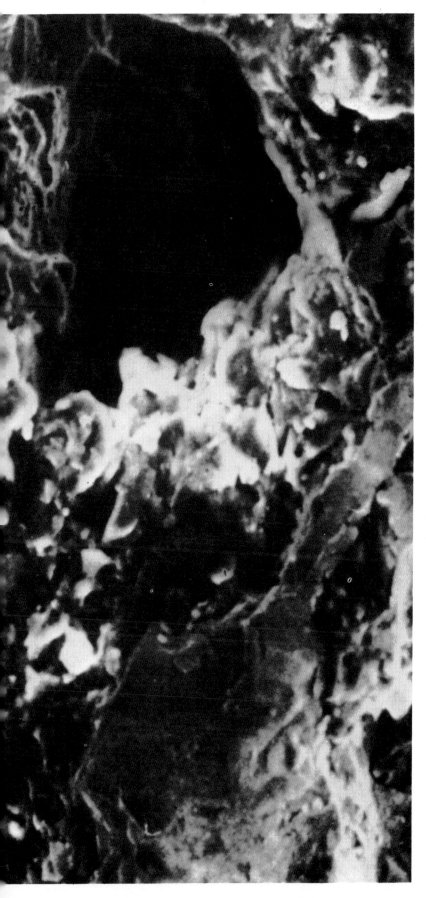

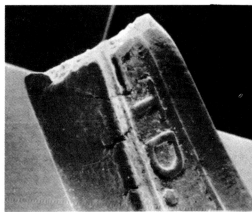

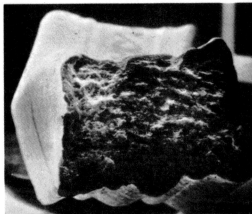

Top: photograph of the fractured
surface of a spoon broken by
Geller's gentle stroking during
his tests with Taylor. Here, the
fracture is seen from the side.
Middle: the fractured surface of
the same spoon, seen head-on.
Above: the same surface, in a
greatly magnified view ($\times 10,000$).
Left: another Geller-fractured
surface, showing the curious cav-
ities and possible indication of
local melting, as if the spoon
had been subjected to intense heat.

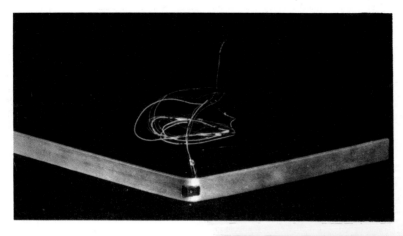

Left: Taylor's ingenious aluminum strip with a pressure sensor set into it so that it could measure the extent of pressure exerted on it. When Geller took it, he did make it bend, but the pressure-sensitive diaphragm crumbled and disintegrated in 10 seconds.

Below: in other Taylor experiments, Geller shattered these crystals without touching them, and distorted the aluminum disks—originally perfectly circular—by holding his hands over them.

Taylor therefore invited a number of young children to his laboratory, and asked them to bend strips of metal and plastic. The results, although not as spectacular as in Geller's case, were fairly startling. Taylor's book *Superminds* (1975) has an interesting assortment of photographs of spoons, forks, and plastic strips bent by children.

But bent spoons and forks are, by their very nature, unconvincing, because even the least skeptical person is likely to suspect that only manual force was involved. This aspect of Taylor's work came in for strong criticism from scientists, particularly when Taylor admitted that some of the bending occurred while he was in the next room. Taylor defended himself by speaking of what he called "the shyness effect"—the fact that bending often occurs when skeptical observers are looking the other way—which provoked the inevitable sarcastic guffaws from his critics. It cannot be denied that Professor Taylor did his case more harm than good by trying to extend it to include other metal benders.

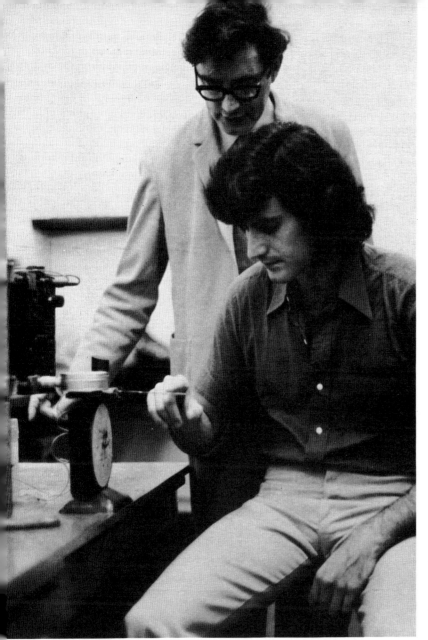

Left: Taylor watches as Geller attempts to bend a metal strip attached to a scale that measures the pressure applied. At no time did Geller's fingers apply more than half an ounce of pressure.

Below: the scale after the experiment. The metal strip bent, but upward, against the pressure of his fingers. Note that the needle of the scale itself also bent.

Immediately after Geller's original appearance on the Dimbleby TV show, *The New Scientist*, the best of Britain's popular scientific journals, carried an editorial recommending that Geller should be studied by scientists. The same opinion was repeated periodically in its pages during the next six months or so. But on October 17, 1974, the day before *Nature* published the Stanford report, it became clear that the editor had experienced a change of heart, or at least a sensible desire to hedge his bets. No less than 16 pages were devoted to an investigation entitled "Uri Geller and Science," most of it written by Dr. Joseph Hanlon, a physicist selected by *The New Scientist* to investigate Geller. Uri had originally agreed to be examined by a *New Scientist* panel that would have included Dr. Hanlon and Dr. Christopher Evans, both of whom were inclined to accept the word of British magicians that Geller was basically a clever conjurer and no more. Warned beforehand to expect skepticism, Geller withdrew his offer. And so, understandably, most of the material used by the

New Scientist was secondhand. It was also totally damning.

Hanlon began his report with both fists swinging: "The whole phenomenon is dominated by Geller's own personality. He exudes sincerity and a childlike innocence and desire to please which makes people really want to like and believe in him. This is reinforced by a high failure rate, which seems to be a constant fear that he will not be able to do what he is trying, and genuine pleasure when he does succeed. And he is a consummate show-man, having been a male model and a stage performer in Israel. On the other hand, even supporters such as Puharich admit that his main goals in life are fame, money, and women, and that he can be childish, petulant, and extremely difficult to work with. It is these latter characteristics that caused ex-astronaut Dr. Edgar Mitchell . . . to fall out with Geller last year. Nevertheless, Mitchell and others who have experienced his whims believe he is one of the most important psychics of our time."

And after this skillful piece of character assassination, Dr. Hanlon proceeds with an analysis of "the magic of Uri Geller" that reads like an abbreviated version of Randi's book (which appeared the following year). In fact, his basic approach is identical to Randi's. Is it more likely that a paranormal event is a fraud or a miracle? Obviously the former. Therefore let us

Left: Alison Lloyd, one of Taylor's young metal benders, who was only 11 years old. She holds her distorted metalware.
Below: a miscellany of bent and broken utensils, produced by several metal benders—most of them children, according to Taylor.

Left: electrodes positioned on the head of a 15-year-old metal bender, to record his brain waves.

Below: the pattern of brain waves recorded. The arrows indicate the moment when the metal bends, but there is no significant abnormality in the child's brain activity.

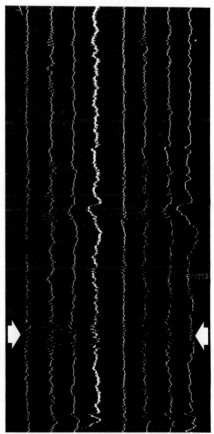

Above: Geller with John Taylor and John Hasted at a press conference in June 1974, when he was in London for a series of tests with Taylor at King's College and Hasted at Birkbeck College.
Below: Geller during the experiments in Birkbeck College with David Bohm, one of the experimenters. At Uri's right is the Geiger counter that clicked loudly when he concentrated on it.

proceed to examine how Geller could have cheated his way through various tests. The argument sounds convincing, but as logic it is abysmal. It is merely saying that the chances are a million to one against a paranormal event happening, which is somewhat like trying to prove that there is no life on earth by arguing that the chances are a million to one against it.

Hanlon cites a number of people who claim to have seen Geller cheating, including a television camera technician who saw him bend a spoon by hand when no one was looking. He even quotes Russell Targ as saying: "I feel confident that Geller will cheat if given a chance." The Stanford experiments were conducted in an atmosphere of chaos—engineered by Geller. But how could Geller have cheated when he got eight out of eight "hits" with a die shaken in a box? How did he locate the film cans that contained ball bearings and similar objects? How did he get such a high score in duplicating drawings? Here Dr. Hanlon comes up with an ingenious hypothesis. It could have been done with the help of Puharich. How? Puharich is an expert in medical electronics, observes Hanlon. It would have been well within his competence to make a radio receiver that would have fitted into one of Uri's teeth, like a filling.

When the *New Scientist* attack appeared, the results of the experiments at Birkbeck College had still not been published. However, Hanlon had succeeded in getting hold of a copy of the Hasted and Bohm report, and although he was violating scientific ethics, he offered a half-page summary of the report. Predictably, the key bending is dismissed very quickly. Hanlon reports that his own tests have shown that anybody can bend a key by holding it in both hands and pressing it against the edge of a chair; he also reports on a session in which Uri succeeded in bending a key, and also in tearing his own overtight jeans, presumably as he tried to lean forward very quickly to bend the key against some solid object. The bent aluminum disk was probably a case of sleight of hand, and as to the Geiger counter's extraordinary behavior, "to me, this is more consistent with Uri or one of his supporters bumping the chart recorder or fiddling with a knob on the amplifier. . . ."

Understandably, Hasted, Bohm, and Bastin were incensed. It is one thing to criticize a paper when it has been published—quite another to offer a highly inaccurate summary and then criticize that. Hasted and Bohm both wrote letters to *The New Scientist*, pointing out that Geller could not have cheated in the way Hanlon suggested. A physicist would have to be particularly stupid not to know the difference between the "chattering" of a Geiger counter and the static noises made by bumping it or fiddling with the controls. And it would be very difficult to perform sleight of hand on a crystal in a sealed container.

And so the controversy dragged on, as it continues to drag on today, and as it no doubt will for the rest of Geller's life. One of the most sensible and useful comments on paranormal phenomena has come from the psychologist Stan Gooch. Gooch pointed out that the cerebrum—the thinking and willing part of the brain—is relatively new; the cerebellum is far older, and seems to be the source of instincts. Man has a double personality, according to Gooch: a conscious Ego and a darker side, associ-

Above: among the objects used in the Birkbeck tests was this single crystal molybdenum disk, which Geller was asked to bend without actually touching the disk himself. It did bend, as shown here. Hasted remarks that this seems to have been the first example of "bending without touching" observed under laboratory conditions.

ated with the cerebellum, that Gooch calls the Self. He suggests that all so-called psychical phenomena are expressions of the Self rather than the Ego, and that if scientists want to try to investigate the Self, they must first recognize the possibility of its existence, and stop behaving as if man were entirely Ego.

Gooch's theory is hardly new; his Self sounds very much like the unconscious, and the Jungian psychologist John Layard had suggested years before that poltergeist phenomena were some form of unconscious activity, taking the form of psychokinesis. But at least Gooch was trying to suggest a fruitful and positive approach to the subject, instead of the drearily negative and barren approach of the skeptics. And his view underlines the basic problem associated with the Geller phenomena. No amount of scientific investigation can prove anything unless the scientist has a *positive theory* into which to fit his observations. Otherwise they are merely unexplained quirks of nature, and nobody can be blamed for ignoring them.

Geller has been investigated by many other scientists besides those in California and London. In 1974, he was investigated in Paris by a commission of scientists led by cybernetician Albert Ducrocq. Geller bent a key, erased the program of a pocket computer, forecast correctly the fall of a die, and demonstrated telepathy; the commission concluded that he was genuine. So did another group of scientists at the Inserm telemetry laboratories at the Foch Hospital, Suresnes, France, the following April. In February 1974, the journal of the American Psychological Association (*Monitor*) produced a positive report on Geller's telepathy by Dr. Edward Kelty. In July 1974, physicists at Western Kentucky University observed Geller deflecting a compass, although he was unable on this occasion to influence a magnetometer. After Geller had left, spoons continued to bend in the house where he had eaten lunch. At Kent State University, in Ohio, Geller was successful in deflecting a magnetometer, and he also scored high in experiments involving a die and film cans, similar to those conducted at the Stanford Institute. In front of television cameras in Toronto, Geller was subjected to various tests by scientists Dr. A. R. G. Owen and his wife Iris Owen; in an article in *New Horizons Journal* Dr. Owen described the conditions as being rigorous as in a laboratory. Both the Owens and the audience were totally convinced by the demonstrations.

But perhaps the most interesting and impressive of the scientific investigations was the one conducted on November 6, 1973 at the US Navy Ordnance Laboratories. This experiment used a strange alloy called Nitinol. Rather like those paper flowers that unfold in water, Nitinol can be squashed completely out of shape, then made to resume its former shape by subjecting it to heat or cold. It has a kind of "molecular memory." Dr. E. Byrd held a piece of Nitinol wire stretched tight between both hands, while Geller stroked the wire. When Geller removed his hand, the wire had a kink in it. Byrd now dropped the wire into boiling water, which should have had the effect of making it snap back into its former shape (the shape in which it was manufactured). In fact, the wire bent into a right angle. Geller had somehow affected its molecular memory. Even melting the wire in a furnace failed to remove the kink.

Right: part of the chart record of the time variation in the magnetic field apparently exerted by Geller's hands as he concentrated in his effort to influence the compass in the Birkbeck tests.

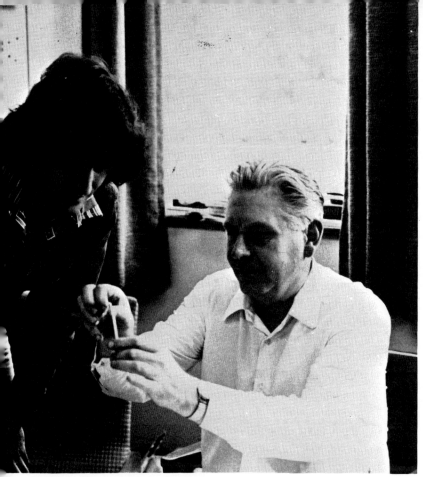

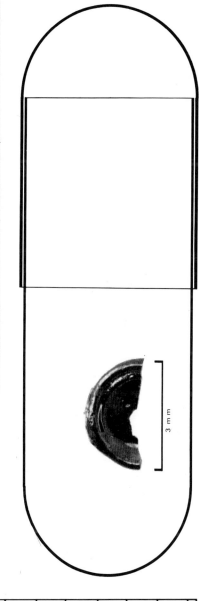

Above: the two Birkbeck College experimenters, Bohm (on the left) and Hasted, with Geller. Hasted is holding a spoon that began to melt and bend in Geller's hand and continued to melt when Hasted took it. It finally broke into two separate pieces.

Right: what was left of the vanadium carbide electron microscope foil after part of it vanished during the tests. It had been enclosed in a sealed plastic capsule, the size and shape of which is indicated here. Hasted put his hand over the capsule, and Uri put his hand on top. Some warmth was apparently generated, and when they checked the foil, half of it had disappeared.

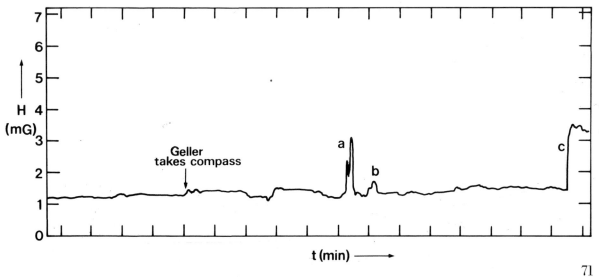

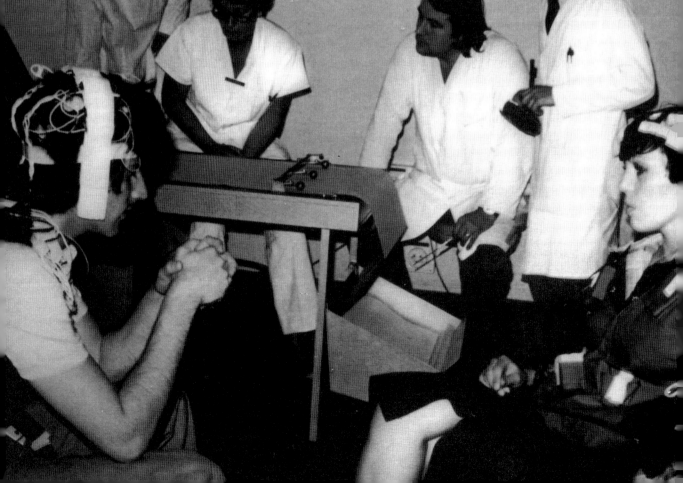

Left: Geller in more laboratory tests, this time with Dr. Albert Ducrocq and his team in France.

No one who reads straight through the various scientific reports on Uri Geller that have been gathered into a book called *The Geller Papers* can doubt that he is more than a mere conjurer with a new gimmick. Critical investigations such as those by Hanlon and Randi carry great weight, partly because most people today find it easier to believe in fraud than in miracles. Also, the things Geller does seem to contradict our everyday experience of the world. But then, as cybernetician Ducrocq has pointed out, the properties of x-rays and radioactivity also contradict our experience of the everyday world, yet they have become the basis of a new type of physics—quantum mechanics.

Let us admit that in a way Geller's powers are thoroughly boring, even if genuine. Bending spoons, repairing watches, and predicting the fall of dice are hardly world-shaking accomplishments. They become important only if they point to something far bigger, to some unknown secret of the universe or of the human mind. Scientists such as Puharich, Mitchell, Bastin, Taylor, Hasted, and Bohm should be given full credit for recognizing this, and risking the inevitable charges of credulousness and naïveté. But so far, none of them has produced even the most tentative outline of some new positive theory that will give us a glimpse of the real significance of the Geller phenomena.

Yet there are already many clues scattered throughout the history of psychical research. Geller is by no means a solitary phenomenon. Let us see whether these scattered clues can be made to yield a fleeting glimpse of the secret that still eludes skeptics and believers alike.

Left: testing during a telepathy experiment, in which Geller tries to receive a thought from a subject selected by the French research team. Both Uri and the girl are wired with electrodes to record the pattern of brain waves.

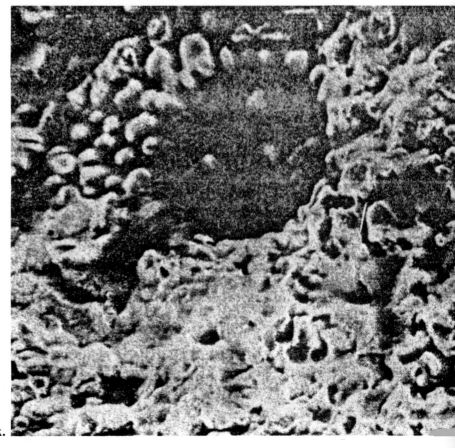

Right: photomicrograph of part of the fracture surface of a ring broken by Geller in the Canadian testing with Dr. A. R. G. Owen. Part of the surface shows signs of melting, but part shows characteristics that seem to suggest some kind of low temperature break.

4

Monsters From the Subconscious?

Rosenheim is a pleasant little manufacturing town on the edge of the Bavarian Alps, some 30 miles southwest of Munich. With its atmosphere of order and tranquillity, it is as unlike modern, frenetic Tel Aviv as one could imagine. Yet it is here, in Rosenheim, that we may find a vital clue to the enigma of the Israeli psychic. In November 1967, strange events began to take place at the office of the lawyer Sigmund Adam, in the Königstrasse. Strip lights exploded so often that a firm of electrical engineers was called in to investigate. They could find nothing wrong, but they replaced the strip lighting with large bulbs. And the explosions con-

The psychologists of the 20th century have accustomed us to the idea of a subconscious level of personality. But the idea that the subconscious mind is capable of acting directly upon matter in the real world still seems incredible, although numerous authenticated cases exist in which that seems to be the most likely hypothesis to explain the facts. Right: one of the few photographs of a poltergeist in action. A stick "jumps" over 14-year-old Yorkshire schoolboy Michael Collindridge, in a Barnsley hotel in 1965.

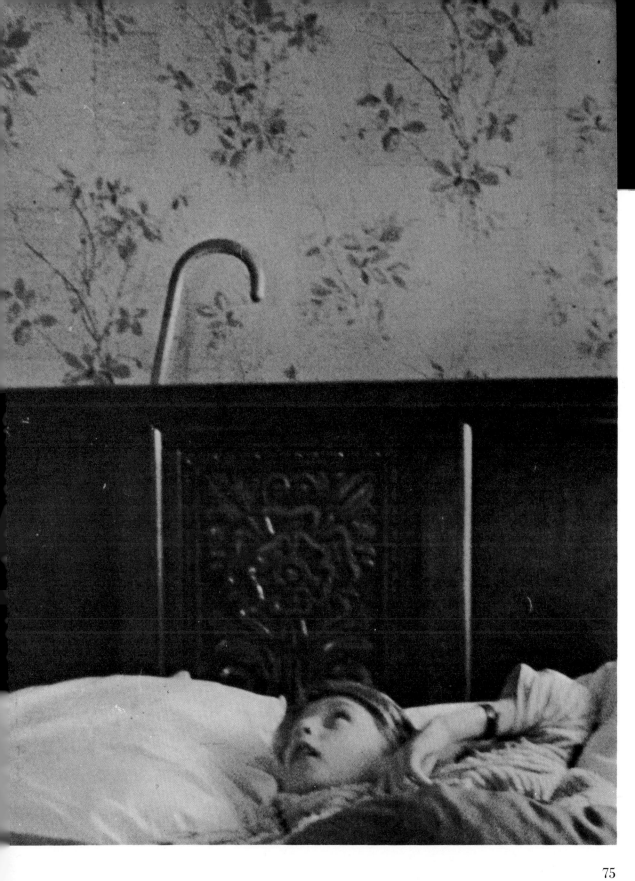

"It was obviously a classic case of poltergeist activity"

tinued. Adam called in the municipal electrical suppliers, who could find nothing wrong. But they placed a special generator in the yard, and ran a cable into the lawyer's office. Still the electrical supply behaved erratically. A voltmeter revealed strange surges of current that were responsible for burning out the bulbs, but no one could explain them.

At this point, Adam began to receive huge telephone bills. A request for detailed accounts revealed that someone had been making hundreds of calls to the service that gives the time, sometimes as many as six a minute. Yet this in itself was absurd, because it took at least 17 seconds to dial the number and get a connection. Even the most determined practical joker could not make more than three calls a minute. Someone—or something—had been getting through direct to the relays.

A reporter came to interview Adam about the odd occurrence. As he was leaving the office after the interview, a neon tube exploded and fell on his head. The reporter's story, entitled "The Rosenheim Spook," was quickly syndicated all over Germany. It was seen by the noted parapsychologist Dr. Hans Bender, who decided to investigate. As one of Bender's assistants was standing in a corridor of the office, he solved the mystery. A young girl was walking down the corridor, and as she passed under the lamps, they began to swing.

Her name was Anne-Marie; she was 19 years old and came from the country. Closer investigation revealed that the surges in the electricity supply occurred only when she was in the office. It was obviously a classic case of poltergeist activity.

Bender's presence seemed to trigger a more normal type of activity. Plates flew through the air, pictures turned on the walls, and a filing cabinet—so heavy that it took two men to shift it—moved several feet away from the wall when no one was near it.

Herr Adam gave Anne-Marie leave of absence to go and be examined at Bender's laboratory in Freiburg. While she was away from the office, everything returned to normal. The moment she came back the disturbances started again. Understandably, Adam fired her. She moved to another office, and the same thing happened there; again she was fired. She took a job in a mill, but her reputation had preceded her. When someone was killed in an accident the whispers began, and Anne-Marie decided to leave.

She was engaged to be married, but this soon came to an end. Her fiancé was fond of bowling at a Roman Catholic youth club. The alley was proud of its electronic equipment: scoring, pin-setting, and return of the balls were all automatic. As soon as Anne-Marie walked in, everything went crazy: the scoreboard registered random scores, and the pins stood up or fell down for no apparent reason. Anne-Marie's fiancé broke the engagement.

There could be no doubt whatever that Anne-Marie was "causing" all these strange occurrences. Yet when Bender first broke the news to her, she was bewildered and incredulous. Even at this point, however, Bender noted a certain ambivalence in her feelings. She was by no means displeased by all the attention.

In his laboratory, he discovered that, like many other Bavarian girls, she had been brought up in a strict Roman Catholic environment, and her father was a stern disciplinarian. Anne-Marie

Left: Anne-Marie Schaberl with her employer, lawyer Sigmund Adam.

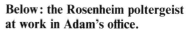

Below: the Rosenheim poltergeist at work in Adam's office.

Left: after Anne-Marie's marriage, the poltergeist activity ended. Many unusual gifts and manifestations cease when adolescence is over, but Geller's powers seem to increase with the years.

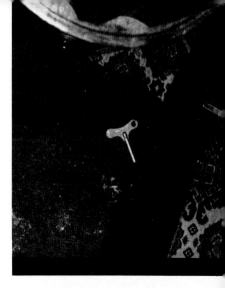

was not a pretty girl; in fact, although she had a certain quiet charm, she was rather plain and ungainly. She had had a number of painful illnesses. And she hated working in a town, especially in an office. Bender concluded that her intense dislike of the office was expressing itself in the form of unconscious psychokinesis. Consciously, she was a mild, kind girl, but her unconscious had all the characteristics of the vandals who wreck telephone booths and slash train seats.

Anne-Marie eventually married another man and had children, and the poltergeist activity stopped. When a BBC team filmed her in 1975, it was clear she was not particularly happy. She felt she had been victimized. But by what? Her own subconscious?

Poltergeists seem completely unpredictable. Records of them date back more than 1000 years, and the general outline of their activities seems vaguely consistent: rappings, bangings, throwing stones, breaking crockery, starting fires. But they also seem to have a bizarre, almost surrealistic, inventiveness. In England in 1662, a poltergeist in the town of Tedworth played a drum all over a house. In the Phelps case, in the United States in 1860, the poltergeist constructed elaborate dummies from clothing. A Barbados poltergeist scattered coffins in a sealed family vault. A poltergeist in Devonshire enjoyed slapping women until they were black and blue. The poltergeist of Barnack Rectory, Northampton, England, specialized in rolling barrels. A Baden-Baden poltergeist drew pictures on windows. And in another case investigated by Bender the poltergeist flooded a certain room with water *from sealed pipes*. This last prank illustrates another fairly familiar aspect of poltergeist behavior: the apparent ability to violate the law of nature that says that two things cannot occupy the same place at the same time. Poltergeists seem to be able to make solid objects pass through brick walls, locked doors, sealed windows, and other barriers. In a case in Croydon, South London, pictures allegedly fell out of their frames without breaking the glass or the sealing at the back of the frame.

The notorious case of the phantom drummer of Tedworth clearly illustrates the link between a poltergeist and a living human being. In 1661, a magistrate named John Mompesson had a vagabond, William Drury, thrown into jail, and confiscated his drum. Violent poltergeist phenomena immediately commenced in Mompesson's house: bangs, thumps, rattlings, and loud tattoos on the drum. The poltergeist also attacked a blacksmith with his own pincers, wrested a sword from a guest and threatened him with it, and pulled a stick out of the hand of a servant woman who was trying to prevent the attack. When William Drury was transported for pig stealing, the disturbances stopped. It seems clear that Drury's violent resentment of the magistrate was somehow able to act at a distance, causing the uproar. This suggests that Drury was able, to some extent, to control his poltergeist. It is also worth noting that the vagabond behind the disturbances was no adolescent, but a full-grown man who had fought under Cromwell.

Despite its apparently human source, a poltergeist often behaves exactly like a demon or mischievous spirit. One of the best-documented is the strange haunting of Esther Cox in the town of Amherst, Nova Scotia in 1878. The disturbances began in the

One well-documented case of poltergeist activity was investigated by the noted English psychical researcher Harry Price around the end of World War II. The activity all appeared to center on an 11-year-old boy, Alan, who lived with his grandmother just outside London. Most of the poltergeist's work was done while Alan was in bed. Above: at midnight on December 22, 1945, during one series of Price's observations, a toy key was found flung to the floor. Above right: at 12:10 a.m. this wrench, which had been kept in the kitchen, dropped on the bedroom floor near the boy's bed. Above far right: at 12:15 a.m. a candle snuffer kept on a chest of drawers appeared on the bed. Right: at 1:00 a.m. the clock from the dressing table fell on the foot of the bed. During these observations the boy had his hands tied to the bed rails with tapes that allowed him to move his hands only about 18 inches. His bed was near the door so that he could summon the investigators as soon as things began happening.

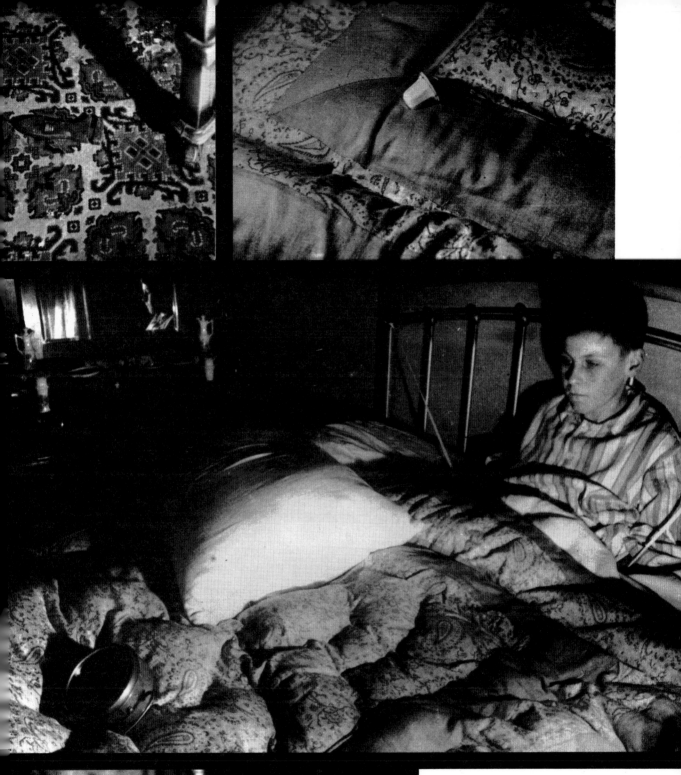

Left: at 1:15 a.m. a trinket case from a dressing table appeared on the bed. The case was not locked, and it seems impossible that Alan could have moved it with his feet—assuming he could have reached it—without spilling everything.

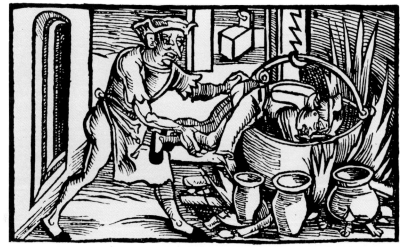

Right: poltergeist in the kitchen, a 1515 woodcut showing a cook being pushed into his cauldron. As early as this, poltergeist phenomena had been recognized and described by baffled observers.

Below: the phantom drummer of Tedworth, a vigorous expression of the bitter resentment of the vagabond William Drury against the magistrate who confiscated his drum and jailed him. The poltergeist activity stopped only when Drury was transported. This 1662 poltergeist is the most reliable early example in England.

house of Daniel Teed, a shoemaker, who lived with his wife Olive and her two unmarried sisters, Jane and Esther. Jane was pretty and had many suitors; Esther was, by comparison, dull and plain. Esther had one boyfriend, a good-looking but violent young man named Bob McNeal. One evening, Bob took Esther for a drive, then tried to persuade her to go with him into the woods. When she refused, he pointed a gun at her and ordered her to accompany him. An approaching rumble of wheels made him change his mind, and he drove her back home at breakneck speed. He left town that night. For the next four days Esther was silent and red-eyed—perhaps regretting her refusal. Then the poltergeist began its disturbances. Esther screamed that a mouse was in bed with her. A box jumped into the air. Then Esther began to flush and to swell up like a balloon. There was a loud explosion, like thunder, followed by three crashes like the report of a gun. Esther returned to her normal size and fell asleep.

The following night, the bedclothes flew around the room and Esther swelled up once more. Again, two loud reports seemed to end the manifestations. A doctor was called in. While he was there, the bedclothes and a pillow again flew around the room, while an invisible hand scratched on the wall the sentence: "Esther Cox, you are mine to kill." This happened with everybody watching it.

Esther complained of a sensation like an electric current in her body. Then new manifestations began. After Esther heard a voice warning her that the house would be set on fire by a ghost, lighted matches began falling from the air. A barrel of wood shavings in the cellar burst into flames and was extinguished with some difficulty.

A kindly neighbor who ran a restaurant offered to take Esther in as a servant. The phenomena now began in his restaurant; there were loud knockings, and objects flew through the air. The poltergeist seemed to prefer metal objects; a clasp knife flew through the air and stabbed Esther in the back, drawing blood, and some heavy iron spokes she was holding suddenly became red-hot. Esther was sacked.

She spent part of the summer in the home of friendly neighbors, and nothing more happened. But when she returned to the Teed cottage, a professional magician had moved in to observe her, and the disturbances began again. Presumably he hoped to catch her cheating, but he was soon convinced that the phenomena were genuine. He persuaded Esther to appear in a public hall to demonstrate her powers. The audience filled the place to capacity, but to their disappointment nothing occurred.

Esther moved back in with the friendly neighbors and the manifestations ceased. She also found a job on a nearby farm. Various articles of clothing vanished from the house where she was staying and reappeared in a barn on the farm; she was accused of theft. Before the case could be pursued, the barn caught fire and burned down. She was sent to jail for four months, accused of arson. The poltergeist now disappeared for good. If it was her unconscious mind that was causing the disturbances, trying to compensate for the loss of her lover by demanding attention, it was now apparently cowed by imprisonment, and gave up its pranks.

Right: the "haunted house" in Nova Scotia where troubled young Esther Cox lived in 1878 when the peculiar happenings began. By the time Esther moved away, the house was almost wrecked.

On the other hand, the open-minded investigator has to admit that perhaps the effects were *not* produced by Esther's unconscious mind, but rather by some kind of mysterious spirit that was able to make use of her energy—and her resentment—to cause havoc. (The Teed cottage was virtually wrecked by the time Esther left.) When we are confronting manifestations as strange as this, no hypothesis can be ruled out. But common sense suggests that for the moment we would do better to accept the simpler and more plausible explanation: that only Esther's subconscious mind, the dark side of her being, was responsible.

Many more cases could be cited, but these three—Anne-Marie, William Drury, and Esther—provide the basic parallels to the Geller phenomena.

The Anne-Marie case is of interest because it demonstrates that her poltergeist (or "Self," as psychologist Stan Gooch calls it) could affect electronic equipment and cause violent surges in an electric current, as well as move heavy objects. Anne-Marie seems to have had no control over the manifestations; in Bender's laboratory, she showed no ability to produce them at will. On the other hand, when Bender began asking her about

Above: a meteorite that was teleported out of a glass container
while Geller was in the house
during a visit to Texas in 1973.
Oddly, the meteorite showed a 10%
weight loss after the episode.

some painful experience connected with her illness, his equipment immediately began to register surges of power from Anne-
Marie. This suggests that, if she had wanted to control the effects,
she might easily have learned the trick of recalling some un-
pleasant event and making herself angry or upset.

From Geller's own book—and from Puharich's—it is clear
that he is only partly able to control his own powers. When I
first went to meet Uri in London, in June 1974, a Spanish coin
jumped out of the ashtray on the desk and fell on the other side
of the room; Geller and a secretary were both on the opposite
side of the room when it happened. And Jesse Lasky, a Hollywood film writer, tells of an occasion when Geller came to dinner
in his apartment in October 1975. The front door of the apartment building he lives in has an iron grill decorated with two
winged dragons. Uri arrived at 8:00 in the evening. At 9:00,
another guest observed the dragons as she came in. When she
left, later on, the wings of both dragons had been bent outward.
Uri had been in the apartment all the time, and was suitably
apologetic about the damage. The caretaker tried to hammer the
wings back but gave up when they began to crack.

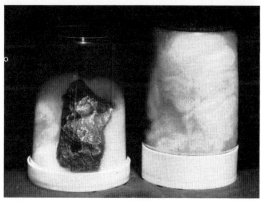

Left: Geller with the meteorite. He had asked to touch it, but it had been resealed into its container afterward. Much later that evening, the meteorite came crashing down in the entrance hall, rooms away from the office-bedroom in which it was kept.

Left: the meteorite as it had been in its case. When it was found in the entrance hall, the owner discovered that the floss on which it had been cushioned had mysteriously fluffed out, completely filling the container. This is another example of the poltergeist phenomena that seem to pursue Geller all the time.

In the Tedworth case it seems quite likely that William Drury deliberately caused the manifestations: he admitted as much to someone who visited him in prison. On his way to transportation to Barbados, he somehow succeeded in escaping: the manifestations immediately began again in the Mompesson household. Here we have a case of a man apparently able to use the "monsters" from his own subconscious to cause damage.

The Esther Cox case also suggests some kind of control—if only minimal—over the phenomena. When she was staying with the friendly neighbors, the manifestations ceased. It was highly convenient for her that the barn burned down before theft could be proved against her. The writing on the wall demonstrates that a poltergeist can "speak." (There have also been many cases that have involved a voice speaking from the air, the first recorded being that of Sir Osborne de Bradaewelle, at Dagworth, in Suffolk, in 1190.) It is a pity that its utterance was confined to that one short sentence: it would have been interesting to know, for example, whether it would have made the same spelling mistakes as Esther.

Anyone who turns to Puharich's book on Uri after reading

about poltergeist cases will immediately be struck by the similar "feel" of the Geller manifestations. Objects are always appearing and disappearing in an erratic manner. There is something oddly trivial about most of the phenomena—car engines stopping and starting, a briefcase "teleported" from America to Israel, a dog mysteriously "dematerialized" and transferred to the other end of the garden. (The same dog later bit Geller, suggesting that it recognized he was the guilty party.) The voice seems to promise important events, but nothing happens. The Space Beings explain that they have come to warn about an Arab attack on Israel, which could become a world war. Puharich did nothing about the warning, and when the next Arab attack occurred, there was, of course, no world war. The Beings explain that they intend to land on earth in the next year or so (this was four years ago), then change their minds and declare that the landing will be "invisible." Yet in another communication they intimate that they are the UFOs that have been reported so frequently, and that have—if we are to believe Ufologists—landed many times. So why make such a fuss about another landing? They explain that their spaceship *Spectra* is "53,069 light ages away," but do not explain why it is necessary to be so far away to help the inhabitants of the earth. After all, the nearest star, Proxima Centauri, is a mere 4.5 light years away. Nor do they explain how they communicate with a spaceship at such a distance, unless they have some form of energy that can travel millions of times faster than light. The contradictions are endless, but are strikingly typical of the "spirit communications" that have occurred so frequently in the history of psychical research. Communicators have often promised—both through automatic writing and through mediums—tremendous philosophical revelations. It would probably be fair to say that most of these revelations never rise above the level of semiliterate double-talk.

Randi, Hanlon, and the rest have no doubt that Geller is cheating, and that Puharich is probably an accomplice. This is simply not consistent with the facts. Before Puharich published *Uri*, no one had cast the slightest doubt on his honesty or his credentials as a scientific investigator of the paranormal. It *might* be argued that Puharich became insane when he met Geller; but again, none of the many people who have interviewed him and talked with him subsequently has expressed any doubts about his sanity. (Since mid-1975, the former close relationship between Geller and Puharich seems to have been subjected to severe strains; but this would appear to be due to Geller's desire to go his own way rather than to any change of attitude on the part of Puharich.)

On the other hand, it is clear that when Puharich met Geller he was already in the frame of mind of a believer—not so much in Geller but in the mysterious "Nine." He went to Israel expecting and hoping for miracles. We have already noted that Uri performs badly in the presence of skeptics. So it would hardly be surprising if Puharich's frame of mind helped to produce some of the extraordinary results of those first weeks in Tel Aviv. In fact, if Uri's powers are derived from his own subconscious mind, is it not perfectly conceivable that these results were due to some kind of collusion between the subconscious minds of the

Above: in another example of poltergeistlike activity on the same evening that the meteorite was teleported, this Imperial Harpa shell emerged from the space in front of a door and whizzed across the room to strike Geller in the back. It normally lay on a tabletop as part of the host's seashell collection. Although it is a very fragile shell, the violent journey did not damage it in any way.

Above: psychic Ray Stanford's car, which he reports was teleported 37 miles when he and his wife were hurrying back to meet Uri at the airport in Austin in 1973. Stanford reports that as they were driving, the scene instantly changed, and they were 37 miles closer to Austin, with no time elapsed and—judging by the gas gauge—no gas consumed, either.

Left: the screened porch at the Puharich home in Ossining, New York, about an hour out of Manhattan, into which Geller reports he was teleported himself on November 9, 1973. He had been on the sidewalk between First and Second Avenue in Manhattan, when he suddenly felt himself propelled through a screen window, crashed through it at a height of eight to 10 feet, and landed inside Puharich's screened porch.

Above: Nandor Fodor, who died in 1964. He was a psychologist and psychic researcher particularly interested in the relationship between psychoanalysis and the paranormal, as (for example) in the case of Mrs. Forbes and the poltergeist of Thornton Heath.

two men? Puharich expected incredible results; he was eagerly awaiting further communication from the Nine. (It would be interesting to know how much he told Geller about the Nine before the metallic voice sounded from the air.) He was a well-known scientist, capable of launching Uri on a world-wide career. What would be more natural than that Uri's subconscious should have gone into top gear to produce spectacular results?

All this suggests that Randi and Hanlon were right and that Uri was indeed cheating, if only on a subconscious level. This is my own opinion, and it is, to some extent, backed by Uri himself, who tells me (on a tape recorded on December 12, 1975): "First of all you must know that I have never agreed to Dr. Puharich's theory, the book that he wrote called *Uri*, where he says that my powers come from outer space and UFOs and Beings and so on. To be quite honest I don't know where this power is coming from. . . ." Yet he has also told me, and many others, that everything Puharich *describes* in his book really happened. When he first met Mitchell, Targ, and Puthoff in 1972, Geller told them that he believed his powers came from Space Beings. It seems incomprehensible that anyone who lived through that year with Puharich, hearing voices speaking from tape recorders and seeing mysterious objects such as UFOs, should completely dismiss the theory that these beings are responsible for his powers. Yet Geller's present attitude is consistent with someone who is aware that Puharich himself was putting much of the "space men" theory into his head, and that his own subconscious powers were acting up to it. It is interesting to compare various accounts of the incident in the Tel Aviv garden when Uri was zapped by the "space man." In Puharich's account, "suddenly between himself and the bowl in the sky there was the shadow of a huge figure like the shadow of a man with a long cape. . . . A blinding ray of light came from its head and struck Uri so forcibly that he fell over backward and into a deep sleep." In Uri's own account in *My Story*, there is only "a silvery mass of light" (not a "bowl-like object") in the sky. "Then it came down lower . . . I felt as if I had been knocked over backward. . . ." No space man emitting a blinding flash of light. In an interview with *Psychic* magazine in 1973, Geller's account is even simpler: "This was the afternoon when I can remember experiencing this flash inside my head as well as outside of it—which was very vivid to me and which seemed to come from up above. I ran to tell my mother about it but she said it was nothing. . . ." This time, apart from the lightninglike flash, the experience sounds much more subjective. It is indeed possible that something happened that afternoon that awakened Uri's powers. But it could well have been something that happened inside his head, some brain discharge, possibly resembling an epileptic attack.

This is, perhaps, the point at which we should discuss the question of the allegations of cheating. Geller himself insists, understandably, that he has never cheated. And his claim is supported by the fact that no one has ever been able to produce evidence that he has cheated, although he has now demonstrated his spoon bending and mind reading many thousands of times. Randi tries hard to imply that Geller was caught cheating, yet fails to produce a shred of evidence in his book. There is, ad-

mittedly, the evidence of people who claim to have seen him
bending spoons manually—such as the TV technician and Randi.
However, Hanlon himself admits in his *New Scientist* article that
hearsay evidence of cheating is as doubtful as hearsay evidence of
miracles. If the technician had filmed Geller bending the spoon
by hand, that would have been a different matter. If Randi and
Charles Reynolds had instantly challenged Geller when—as they
allege—they saw him press the key against the tabletop, this,
too, would have been worth taking seriously. But even allowing
that Randi and Reynolds were totally honest, we still have to
acknowledge that they were hoping to catch Geller cheating, and
that their perception could have been influenced by wishful
thinking.

So there is no hard evidence that Geller has ever cheated; and
if his powers are as unusual as they seem to be, it is difficult to see
why he should endanger his reputation by cheating. His supporters have occasionally pointed out that many genuine
mediums have been known to cheat, in order to provide "value
for money" when their powers are weak—an admission that has
drawn predictable boos and catcalls from the opposition. If
Targ's remark that he believes Uri would cheat if he got the
chance is authentic, then he clearly takes the view that Uri is both
genuine *and* capable of trickery. This possibility has to be frankly
acknowledged—while still bearing in mind that there is no real
evidence that Uri has even helped out his powers by sleight of
hand.

This is not to suggest that the skeptics are wrong to look for
trickery—only that their skepticism is based on a naive and
simple-minded attitude. Their basic belief is that such powers
cannot exist, according to their preconceived ideas about the
universe. They are committed to the view that all mediums and
psychics are frauds; consequently, if one of them is caught cheating, this is a clear and logical proof of their contention. It is never
as simple as that. This emerges very clearly in one of the classic
books of psychical research, Nandor Fodor's *On the Trail of the
Poltergeist*. Fodor was a Freudian psychologist who was inclined
to the view that psychic manifestations are often explosions of
subconscious energy. In 1938, Fodor was called in to investigate
a case at Thornton Heath, in south London. The woman at the
center of the disturbance was a housewife; Fodor calls her "Mrs.
Forbes." On the day Fodor first called on her, accompanied by
another doctor, objects sailed through the air, a glass flew from
her hand and exploded in mid-air as if struck by a hammer, and
things vanished from in front of their eyes and appeared elsewhere. A saucer apparently passed through a closed door. At
investigations in the laboratory, all kinds of objects fell from the
air: pottery, coins, lamps, even white mice and a bird. In the car,
as they drove home afterward, the lid of a box opened and closed
of its own accord as Fodor stared at it. Mrs. Forbes sometimes
claimed that a tiger was clawing at her. Those around her smelled
a fetid odor like that of a zoo, and claw marks were found on her
body. At this point, an x-ray examination revealed that she had
concealed some small objects in her vagina. It looked, then, as if
she was a fraud. Yet the evidence was strongly against this. Once,
in her house, she asked Fodor what object he would like her to

Above: Victorian medium Daniel Dunglas Home. The most famous physical medium, Home produced a wide range of phenomena that included levitation and partial materialization. He worked in full light, and was never caught in any kind of trickery or fraud.

Right: one of Home's levitations.

"materialize." He replied: a Roman lamp, this time of terra cotta. (She had materialized a Roman lamp before.) A few minutes later, he went into her bathroom and found a fragile lamp of terra cotta.

In some of her convulsions, Mrs. Forbes swelled up as if her stomach were a balloon. (Esther Cox had done the same thing.) She experienced hysterical blindness, and produced stigmata such as "tiger scratches" while witnesses were watching her. One day, when Fodor was walking with her, she opened her handbag, took out a stone, and threw it over her shoulder; when Fodor asked why she had done this, she indignantly denied it. She had apparently done it without even being aware of it.

Fodor concluded that Mrs. Forbes's various problems and

ailments (she had suffered much illness, physical and mental, before the manifestations began) were due to some sexual trauma. He was not allowed to complete his investigation (psychical researchers at this time felt that the Freudian suggestions were indecent), but was fairly convinced that the origin of her problems may have been an attempted rape, possibly by her father.

Was Mrs. Forbes genuine or a fraud? Both. It is impossible to draw some clear line and state exactly where the real manifestations ended and fraud began. It is doubtful if Mrs. Forbes herself knew. Fodor observed: "As a woman who produced miracles, she felt she had a position to maintain. This position had liberated her from the dull life of a suburban housewife. . . ." Yet to dismiss her as a fraud would be a crude oversimplification. More than that: it would amount to scientific dishonesty. For Mrs. Forbes's frustration produced effects that were apparently against the normal laws of nature. And until they can be explained, they remain a challenge to science.

There is one obvious basic difference between Mrs. Forbes and Uri Geller, and it also happens to be a difference between two kinds of psychic. Mrs. Forbes's powers were the result of mental strains; so were Anne-Marie's and Esther Cox's. In the mid-19th century, certain investigators of the paranormal liked to talk about "sick sensitives," and the description certainly fits this type of psychic. On the other hand, Geller obviously belongs to a different group of psychics who are basically healthy and in most ways normal. Their powers seem to be some kind of freak, in the way that some people are born double-jointed, or with the ability to hear sounds beyond the normal human range.

As we have seen, the subconscious mind can, and often does, produce violent paranormal phenomena. In the case of most healthy psychics, the phenomena are usually less violent, yet just as inexplicable in normal terms. Few psychics can control them completely, although some have more control than others.

It is important to realize that Uri Geller is a far from unique phenomenon. From the phantom drummer of Tedworth to the present, there have been literally dozens who have produced effects just as strange and baffling as Geller's. Let us look more closely at this second type of psychic.

Perhaps the most famous of all was the Victorian medium Daniel Dunglas Home, who could cause chairs and tables to float up to the ceiling, wash his face in red-hot coals, and float in and out of second-story windows. Home was so certain of his powers that he usually insisted on demonstrating them in well-lighted rooms. Dozens of respectable scientists, clergymen, and eminent people observed his performances under these conditions and signed affidavits as to their genuineness.

The foremost Victorian scientific investigator of the paranormal, Sir William Crookes, conducted a series of sittings with Home under what he regarded as test conditions, and published the results in several classic papers. On April 11, 1871, Crookes prevailed on Home to collaborate with a medium called Herne in a seance in the dark. At first, he says, the manifestations were "rough"; the table floated into the air and crashed down noisily, and they were surrounded by coarse, bawling voices. After Home began to sing a hymn, "Mr. Herne was carried right up,

Above: Sir William Crookes, with "Katie King," a spirit materialization of the medium Florence Cook, with whom Crookes worked in a lengthy series of experiments. He was trained as a physicist, but became the best-known investigator of the seance room. His work with Home convinced him of the reality of spirit phenomena, but publication of his findings exposed him to scientific attack.

floated across the table and dropped with a crash of pictures and ornaments at the other end of the room. My brother Walter, who was holding one hand, stuck to him as long as he could, but says Herne was dragged out of his hand as he went across the table." Voices—pleasant ones this time—spoke around them. One sitter observed a hand removing a book from the table, and he grabbed it; it proved to be a disembodied hand, which carried the book across the table. Hands picked up an accordion and played it in mid-air. (On another occasion, Crookes watched the accordion being played by invisible hands while it was completely enclosed in a cage.)

Home himself had no doubt that these phenomena were caused by spirits of the dead. (This, of course, applies to most mediums.) But investigators such as Crookes and Professor Charles Richet, although totally convinced of the genuineness of the phenomena, were not necessarily convinced that the dead were responsible. They already suspected that some hidden part of the mind can play extraordinary tricks. Richet, a distinguished chemist, concluded sensibly: "The more I reflect and weigh in my mind these materializations, hauntings, marvelous lucidity [ESP and "second sight"], apports [objects that fall out of the air], xenoglossia [speaking in strange tongues], apparitions and, above all, premonitions, the more I am persuaded that we know absolutely nothing of the universe that surrounds us."

For the ability to reproduce drawings sealed in envelopes, Richet invented the word "cryptesthesia." His *Thirty Years of Psychical Research* contains many pages describing his investigations into cryptesthesia with various amateur psychics, and shows sketches and target drawings that are as striking as Geller's. He wrote: "In certain persons, at certain times, there exists a faculty of cognition which has no relation to our normal means of knowledge." He later called this faculty "the sixth sense."

Apart from Home, there have been many remarkable mediums whose claims have been investigated by scientists, including Mrs. Leonore Piper, Eusapia Paladino, Rudi Schneider, Eileen Garrett, and Ena Twigg. Mrs. Piper, like Uri Geller, received her first intimation of strange powers when she was playing in a garden as a child. Something struck her on the ear, and a voice said: "Aunt Sara is not dead, but with you still." It later turned out that Aunt Sara had died at that exact moment. Shortly after this incident, the child's bed rocked violently from side to side one night, and the room was full of a strange light that prevented her from sleeping. As an adult she became a medium, and was noted for the remarkable accuracy of the information she was able to give about dead relatives of her sitters. Scientists arranged all kinds of rigorous test conditions to make sure she was not cheating. One had her followed by a private detective for days before a sitting; another tried the experiment of sending her to a foreign country—England—of which she knew little, engaging a completely new staff of servants to look after her, and forbidding her to read newspapers; still, her information during seances remained copious and accurate.

In view of the impressive testimony of men of science and philosophy—including Sir Oliver Lodge and William James— there seems to be no doubt of the genuineness of her powers. There remains the possibility that she may have possessed very unusual powers of telepathy, enabling her to pick up her information from other minds. She herself said, "Spirits of the departed may have controlled me and may have not. I confess that I do not know." Whatever the origin of her powers, they survived several decades of the most rigorous testing that scientists could devise.

A medium whose powers are considerably closer to Uri Geller's is the famous Lajos Pap, a woodcutter from Budapest, who was in his late 30s when he first accidentally attended a seance. The sitters held a heavy table to the ground by pressing their feet on the bottom of its legs; yet the force being exerted was so great that it loosened the massive tabletop and made it rise into the air. A process of elimination revealed Pap to be the one who was responsible. Five years later, Pap produced his first apports—an ability for which he became famous. A wild flower and a tobacco pouch fell onto the table in a locked room. Obviously, the first question to be asked in such a case is whether the medium has concealed them in his pockets. Lajos Pap convinced one scientist when a cross weighing 20 pounds fell from the air. In seances, with his hands and feet held and even his mouth sealed, Lajos was able to apport flowers, stones, insects, a dead squirrel, birds, fish, mice, bottles, and showers of wine, beer, black coffee, cream, and liqueur—what kind is not specified.

Nandor Fodor tested Lajos in Budapest. In a locked laboratory, Pap was thoroughly searched, then made to don a garment that covered him from neck to feet (presumably so he could

Above: the remarkable Bostonian medium Mrs. Leonore Piper, who was discovered by William James. She was investigated for 30 years by British and American workers.

The document apport.

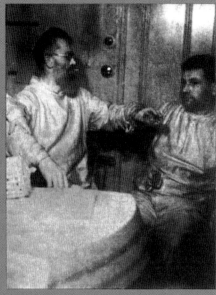

Ectoplasmic cigarette.

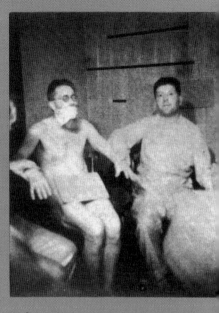

French 1875 gold coin apport.

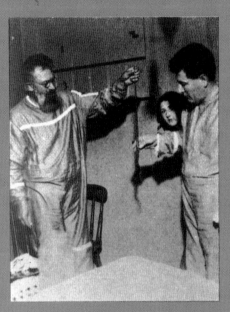

The dead snake after the seance.

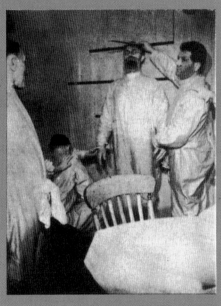

Pap's attempt at elongation.

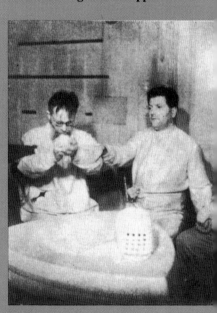

Handkerchief ectoplasm.

Above: six photographs taken in the course of the Lajos Pap seances at the International Institute for Psychical Research. During these seances Lajos purported to produce (from left to right, top row) documents, an ectoplasmic cigarette, a gold coin—the medium being naked at the time—and (bottom row) a 28-inch snake, elongation of his own body, and an ectoplasmic handkerchief. Nandor Fodor concluded that the handkerchief was certainly fraudulent, and there were grounds for suspicion of fraud with all the other apports produced in London. But he did feel that the results Lajos had earlier obtained in Budapest were worthy of further intensive scientific investigation. Right: the garment that Lajos wore during the tests, with phosphorescent bands to reveal any of the medium's movements.

not, like Mrs. Forbes, use natural orifices to conceal things). Pap's hands and feet were held, but he was still able to make slight scooping motions in the air with his hands. In this way he collected 30 beetles—all alive and protesting—and twigs of acacia, wild rosebuds, and a four-inch cactus plant. On another occasion, Fodor watched Pap cause a basket painted with luminous paint to float around the room, at the height of his hands, and obey his orders. Typically, Fodor dismissed this demonstration because Pap could have been somehow controlling it with an invisible thread. Yet he was totally convinced by the living apports. Fodor had been a collector of insects, and knew the immense difficulty of catching dragonflies and of handling stag beetles without getting bitten. Pap produced many dragonflies, and on one occasion 15 stag beetles. If these had been somehow concealed on him (he was almost naked under the robe), his chances of getting bitten were considerable.

When Pap came to London in 1935, he produced much the same kind of sensation as Uri Geller, and might have produced even more if television had existed then. On this occasion, Fodor came to the conclusion that many of the apports—including a dead poisonous snake—could have been fraudulent, simply because he judged that Pap had the opportunity to conceal various objects on his person. Yet he concludes: "Nor would I be willing to declare him a fraud and nothing but a fraud. Too long has psychical research been the victim of the fatal delusion that a medium is either genuine or fraudulent." He goes on to add a fascinating comment that may throw a new light on the problem

Below: the arrangement of the seance room for the Lajos tests. The medium's chair is indicated by the circle marked with an M. The room was liberally furnished with cameras, thermometers, and luminous slates on the walls.

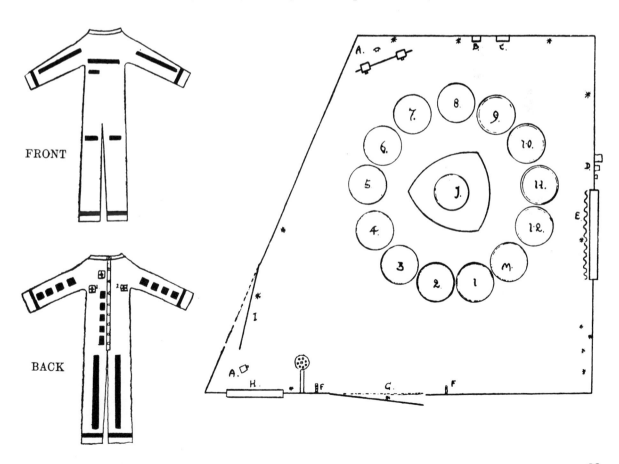

FRONT

BACK

of the poltergeist. "It is a minimal assumption that mediumship means a dissociation of personality. There was plenty of evidence that Lajos Pap was suffering from such dissociation." He believed that Pap was a kind of Jekyll-and-Hyde personality. Many famous cases of dual personality have been studied by psychologists. Perhaps the most widely known is the "three faces of Eve" case written about by Thigpen and Cleckley. The subject was a suburban housewife who was periodically taken over by a completely different personality that led her into many embarrassing situations. Geller himself shows no obvious signs of a dual personality; yet it may be significant that the voices from the air began to sound as soon as he was under hypnosis, just as many mediums are taken over by their "spirit guide" as soon as they go into a trance.

Since World War II, a number of highly gifted psychics have been tested by scientists and pronounced genuine. Two of the most widely publicized are Gerard Croiset, a Dutch clairvoyant, and Peter Hurkos, another Dutchman, who lives in the United States. Both these men possess the same kind of second sight that Mrs. Piper displayed, and both have used them to help the police solve murder cases. Hurkos's powers developed during the war, when he fell off a ladder and suffered concussion. When he recovered, he found himself unable to concentrate on the normal tasks involved in making a living; by way of compensation, he had acquired an ability to know about events that had taken place elsewhere or at other times. His "psychic radar" seems to operate when he handles various objects associated with these events. In a typical case, Hurkos was asked by the police to sit in the taxicab of a murdered driver. Hurkos gave a careful description of a man whose name, he said, was "Smitty," and who had also, said Hurkos, been responsible for another death—of a naval man shot in his apartment. The police were astonished; there had been such a murder recently, but they had not connected it with the cabdriver's death. A waitress reported a conversation with a drunken sailor who boasted of killing two men; at the police station, she picked out a photograph of a sailor named Charles Smith. A "wanted" notice went out for him, and he was arrested in New Orleans. Smith confessed to the cabdriver's murder and was sentenced in 1958. Hurkos had described "Smitty" accurately even to a tattoo on his arm.

I had occasion, in 1975, to interview Gerard Croiset, a clairvoyant of Utrecht, for BBC television. The subject of the interview was a girl named Pat Macadam, who had vanished while hitchhiking from Glasgow. When the driver who had given her a lift was located, he claimed that he had dropped her off near her home. He had a police record for sexual assaults, and was shortly afterward sent to prison for another. Finally, the driver admitted that he had turned off the main road when driving Pat home and said that he and Pat had had sexual relations before they drove on. His story could not be disproved, and he was released. However, a local journalist went to visit Croiset in Utrecht and took Pat's Bible. Croiset held it, and unhesitatingly declared that Pat was dead. She had been killed in the course of an attempted sexual assault, and her body thrown from a nearby bridge. He described the bridge, and also an adjacent

Above: Gerard Croiset, the Dutch sensitive, who has become famous through his successful work in tracing lost people and objects.

Right: Peter Hurkos, the Dutch psychic who first developed his powers after an accident in which he suffered a concussion. He now lives in the United States, and has worked with many police departments to trace missing persons.

Above: Ingo Swann, an American artist and psychic, who has worked with several researchers studying the nature of his powers. Perhaps the most fascinating results have been from tests of "out-of-body experiences," in which Swann, observably sitting in one place, has produced information hidden in completely inaccessible spots.

house with advertisement signs on it, and a disused car in the garden, with a wheelbarrow propped against it. Police discovered the bridge, and the house with the disused car and the wheelbarrow propped against it, exactly as Croiset had described. If Pat's body had indeed been thrown from the bridge, her killer was lucky; the river was subject to sudden violent flooding, and the body had almost certainly been carried out to sea. The case remains unsolved. Yet no one who has seen Croiset's drawings of the places associated with Pat's death and then visited the sites themselves could have the slightest doubt that Croiset possesses astonishing powers of second sight.

Equally remarkable, although less widely known, is the Swedish psychic Olof Jonsson, who has also been extensively tested by scientists. The most spectacular story about Jonsson concerns a particularly horrifying series of murders that took place in Sweden in 1952; in all, 13 people were murdered, mostly shot and their houses set on fire. A journalist friend asked Jonsson to help. The police obligingly took the psychic from one scene of crime to another, and he correctly described what had happened. Then, as a police officer named Hedin handed him a burned rifle, Jonsson suddenly knew with certainty that this man was the murderer, and that the crimes were committed for robbery to buy gifts for a demanding mistress. Before Jonsson could convince the police of Hedin's guilt, the policeman had committed suicide, leaving a note confessing to the murders.

In America in 1966, Jonsson agreed to help in another case that looked like sex murder; three young girls had disappeared after a trip to the India dunes region near Chicago; the car of one of them was found abandoned in the dunes park. Jonsson handled cigarettes belonging to the girls, and declared that they were still alive; they had bleached their hair, he said, and were living in the town of Saugatuck, in Michigan. On the urgings of the parents of one of the girls, Jonsson went to Saugatuck and located a waitress and doorman who could identify photographs of the girls. All three were found alive.

Jonsson's remarkable ESP powers have been extensively tested by scientists; his score in card and dice guessing tests is as consistently high as Geller's. He has often revealed a gift for foretelling the future; he accurately predicted the time and place of the deaths of de Gaulle and Nasser.

A few months before Geller was tested at Stanford, a New York artist and psychic named Ingo Swann was also able to deflect the needle of a shielded magnetometer under strict test conditions. But this is one of the least of Swann's abilities. Swann belongs to a group of psychics who claim to possess the power known as "traveling clairvoyance"—the ability to leave the physical body and project the spirit (or "astral body") elsewhere. This, too, was tested by Hal Puthoff and Russell Targ. Swann was locked in a room at the Institute; then the experimenters threw dice, and looked up the number corresponding to the result in a locked filing cabinet, which contained a set of numbered cards. The card thus selected by chance bore instructions to drive to Palo Alto Town Hall. Once there, Targ and Puthoff tried to transmit their impressions of the place, which included a crossroads, two trees, and a dry fountain. When they returned,

Swann had done an accurate drawing showing the crossroads, and the trees, and a note about the fountain.

Before the *Mariner 10* spacecraft set out for Jupiter and Mercury, Swann and another psychic, Harold Sherman, decided that this would be an ideal opportunity to test their powers of long-distance projection. Accordingly, they attempted to project themselves to these planets. Their impressions were written down, then examined by a lawyer and notarized. When the spacecraft sent back its reports on the planet, Swann and Sherman eagerly compared these with their own impressions. Their description of Jupiter, they admit, was only partly accurate; but their impressions of Mercury were phenomenally accurate. Swann had not only mentioned Mercury's magnetic field, but also described the precise shape of the field, as reported by *Mariner 10*.

Swann claims that it took him only eight minutes to locate Mercury, from which we may deduce that astral travel is almost as fast as light. This may explain how Puharich's "Nine" can project themselves over 50-odd light years of space. All this, of course, sounds absurd—except that Swann and Sherman have the dated, notarized documents to prove the accuracy of their description of Mercury.

Ingo Swann prefers to call his peculiar faculty "remote viewing" rather than astral travel, which has overtones of nuttiness. The same is true of Pat Price, the subject who shares Targ and Puthoff's report with Uri Geller. Price is a former California police commissioner and city councilman. Understandably, most of the attention received by the article was directed at Uri, because he happened to be by far the more controversial of the two. Yet if we accept the findings of Targ and Puthoff, Price scored as consistently as Geller. The method was basically the same as in the tests with Ingo Swann: a location was chosen (from a pool of 12) by some random method, and one experimenter remained with Price, asking him for his impressions, while the others drove to the spot chosen as the target. This was done nine times, and six of Price's descriptions were so accurate that an independent team of judges was able to "match up" the actual place against the transcript of Price's words.

This ability, whether called "remote viewing" or "astral travel," is by no means rare. Many books have been devoted to it, and in recent years scientifically controlled tests like the ones at Stanford have begun to produce an impressive body of documentation. The point it underlines is that Geller, far from being a unique figure, is only one of hundreds of gifted psychics, whose faculties merely happen to be less newsworthy than his own. One of them is a young British psychic, Matthew Manning, whose powers seem to be quite as extraordinary as Geller's.

In February 1967, Matthew's father, a Cambridge architect, came down to breakfast and found his favorite silver tankard on the living room floor. No one in the family could explain how it got there. A few days later, the tankard again fell off the shelf in the night. Suspecting a joke, Matthew's father surrounded the tankard with talcum powder; the next morning, the powder was undisturbed, but the tankard was again on the floor. Dr. George Owen, a Cambridge expert on poltergeists, was called in to investigate, and he quickly concluded that they were dealing with a genuine member of this mischievous fraternity. A wooden chair was overturned, an armchair moved six feet, a candlestick was thrust into a vase of flowers. Dr. Owen concluded that Matthew—then aged 11 and the only Manning child near puberty—was the unconscious force behind the poltergeist.

After three months, the manifestations stopped—as poltergeist manifestations usually do. Four years later, they began again, in a manner that recalls the famous Douglass Deen case, on which the book *The Exorcist* was based. Matthew's bed rose into the air and shook. A heavy settee was moved across his bedroom door. From then on, the Mannings came down each morning to new scenes of chaos: furniture would be strewn around the rooms or piled up in a heap. At one point a broom balanced itself on the banister. The house was filled with thuds and pinging noises.

Matthew became a boarder at Oakham School. There the manifestations continued, to such an extent that the headmaster twice requested Matthew's removal, although he relented on both occasions. Then the poltergeist phenomena suddenly ceased, as Matthew developed another aspect of his psychic abilities. Since the age of 15, he had occasionally practiced "automatic writing"; now his hand showed a talent for automatic drawings—not the usual childish scrawls produced by amateur psychics, but talented carefully executed drawings in such diverse styles as those of Picasso, Dürer, Beardsley, and Beatrix Potter. Sometimes there were inscriptions on these drawings in languages Matthew could not understand. Messages in Latin, French, and Arabic appeared mysteriously on the drawings. Like Arigó, Matthew was sometimes taken over by the spirit of a dead doctor, who was able to make startlingly accurate medical diagnoses of visitors at a single glance, as well as prescribing remedies. In January 1974, when Matthew watched Uri Geller bending spoons on television, he tried it himself and instantly succeeded. The scientist Dr. Joel Whitton testified to seeing a spoon bend when Matthew was not even touching it.

Like Uri, Matthew has told his own story, in a book called *The Link*. Like Uri, he has been extensively investigated by scientists, who have testified to the genuineness of the phenomena. He differs from Geller in one basic respect; he has no desire to make money from his gifts or to demonstrate them in front of large audiences, although he did appear once on television, on the David Frost program. "Uri Geller did a lot of good, but also a lot of damage," he once told a reporter, and added: "I don't want to be looked at. Psychics cannot perform at the drop of a hat. Basically, it's like running a battery. You use it up, and have to wait. . . . Besides, it's exhausting." And so the quiet, introspective Manning continues to live in Cambridge, shunning publicity, and collaborating with scientists who wish to investigate his powers.

Here we have a well-documented case of poltergeist phenomena developing into more diverse and sophisticated psychic powers. Yet we still lack an explanation for the phenomena. How do we account for the drawings in so many styles, for the writing in Latin and Arabic? Yet we can make at least one statement

Above: Matthew Manning, a young English psychic. Now in his 20s, Manning first became aware of his powers when his family was plagued by a rash of poltergeist activity, and Oxford researcher Dr. George Owen concluded that it was probably Manning supplying the unconscious force behind the manifestations. The poltergeist activity stopped as he developed powers of automatic writing and drawing, and—inspired by a TV program showing Geller at work— he immediately discovered that he had the power to bend metals.

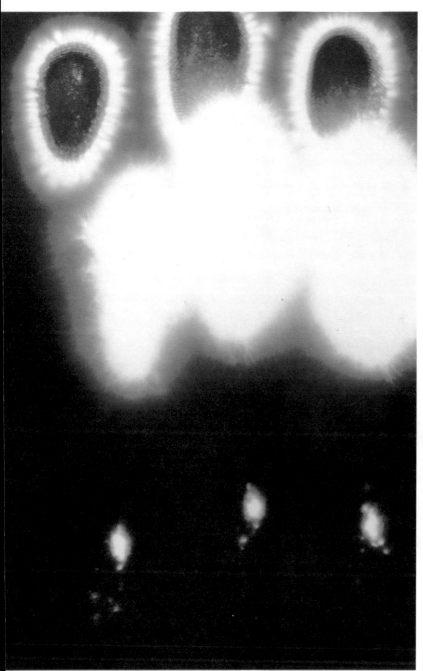

Left: three Kirlian photos of Manning's fingertips. The top picture shows his fingers at rest, and the result is already somewhat stronger than the radiation produced by the average person. In the middle panel are the photos taken when he was asked to "turn the power on," and at the bottom is the result of a request to focus the energy to a pinpoint.

Above: EEG readings taken on Manning during tests at the New Horizons Research Foundation in Toronto, which showed that during his metal-bending efforts he registered a remarkable amount of low frequencies on the machine.

Left: Manning with Dr. Karlis Osis, director of the American Society for Psychical Research, who was in Toronto for the tests.

Left: Manning drawing a "Picasso." In 1971, with the automatic writing well established, Manning's mother suggested he might try drawing, by asking that a dead artist might draw a picture using Manning's hand. Below left: a finished "Picasso." About three months after Picasso's death Manning produced the first drawing in his characteristic bold strong style. Unlike the other artist communicators, who prefer to use black ink only, Picasso frequently works in colors.

MATTHAVS LANG VON WELLENBVRG

1522

Above: a Manning "Dürer" portrait, dated 1522, with the sitter's name.

Right: another "Dürer" portrait, this one dated 1503. Manning notes that many of these portraits are obviously reproductions of drawings that Dürer was known to have produced during his lifetime.

Above: a splendidly prickly Dürer porcupine, signed with the artist's distinctive monogram.

with reasonable confidence: if poltergeists are manifestations of the unconscious, then Matthew's powers emanate from the depths of his own mind. He has said as much in a letter to me: "I feel that these powers are basically of a poltergeist nature albeit on a more controlled level. I believe that the mind or brain generates what we term a 'psychic energy,' and that this can be applied to producing physical phenomena. . . ." As to the possible source of his powers, he has also mentioned, in a letter to me, that his mother sustained a violent electric shock when she was carrying him. This is an interesting parallel with Geller, who received a shock as a boy, while his mother was sewing.

Perhaps the most fascinating aspect of the recent publicity given to Uri Geller's psychic abilities is that so many people have become aware that they too possess such powers. John Taylor's spoon-bending children have made him the target of a great deal of skepticism and even derision. It is possible, and indeed probable, that some of them bent spoons in the normal way by hand when Taylor's back was turned. Yet no one who has read with an open mind Taylor's account of some of the test conditions can doubt that some of the phenomena must have been genuine. Moreover, the "Geller effect" has been observed in almost every country where his abilities have been demonstrated on television. Following his visit to Japan in 1973, so many Japanese children showed ability to bend spoons, start watches, recharge dead batteries, and predict the future that many scientists started to study them. Shigemi Sasaki, professor of psychology at Denki Tsuchin University in Tokyo, formed a team of 15 investigators and set out to explore the PK (psychokinetic) abilities of children. He enclosed a piece of wire horizontally in a glass dome, with a small weight on it to give it a certain downward tension, and then asked a succession of children to hold their hands near it and attempt to bend it. Kenji Hashimoto, former professor of engineering at Tokyo University, was astounded as he watched the wire bend steadily downward, and he declared afterward that it was impossible for it to have been done by trickery. One unusually talented 12-year-old, Jun Sekiguchi, not only bent three spoons, one after another, merely by holding them in full view of the scientists, but was apparently able to dematerialize part of the metal; 0.03 of a gram had been lost when one spoon was reweighed. Dr. Sasaki has also described the abilities of a 15-year-old called Satoshi (his parents wanted his identity kept secret). Besides bending metal, Satoshi also showed extraordinarily accurate powers of prediction. He correctly foretold two earthquakes and their location, and also predicted the financial scandals that caused the resignation of the then Prime Minister, Kakuei Tanaka.

Geller seems to possess remarkable ability to induce psychic powers in other people; but this may be due to the fact that more people have seen him on television than have seen, for example, Ted Serios or Ingo Swann. Most dowsers (water diviners) will tell you that they can teach people to dowse; but they will also admit that the faculty is latent in all of us, and that it is simply a matter of "tuning in." Felicia Parise, an attractive 37-year-old New Yorker who works as a leukemia researcher in a New York hospital, was so intrigued by films of the Soviet psychic Nina

BILIBALDI · PIRKEYMHERI

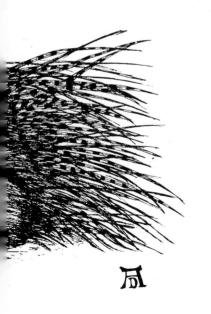

Above: one of the metal-bending children cited by Professor John Taylor—Mark Shelley, then seven years old—exhibits the bent cutlery he produced imitating Geller.

Right: Russell Jennings, then 12 years old, who was one of Taylor's best metal-bending subjects, with his autographed picture of Geller.

Kulagina, who can move objects on a tabletop by staring at them, that she decided to try it herself. Soon she found that she was able to make small objects slide around on a smooth tabletop simply by staring and concentrating. Her abilities were examined under test conditions at Duke University by Dr. Graham Watkins, who confirmed her ability to move a compass needle by concentrating on it. Dr. Charles Honorton, at New York's Maimonides Institute, observed her moving a small bottle on a tabletop by PK. Dr. Christopher Evans included shots of her moving a glass on a tabletop in a television film he made about paranormal research. Other scientists have confirmed her ability to move pieces of tinfoil enclosed in a bell jar, create an energy field that can influence electrical instruments, cause unexposed film to fog over by concentrating on it, and achieve billion-to-one scores in receiving mental images transmitted to her by researchers. But she admits "After only five or ten minutes of concentrating, I'm exhausted. I perspire freely; sometimes my nose and eyes run. I tremble. It

Left: another young metal bender, June Charlton, bends her father's pipe while he is trying to smoke.

Below: another of Taylor's metal-bending children, a girl of 13, was able to bend metal objects at a distance and also showed considerable ability at telepathy, producing the drawings at the right in response to the targets shown at the left. All three were drawn outside the room where the child sat, but transmitted by a person sitting in the same room.

takes a tremendous physical effort—such an effort that I can hardly speak afterwards. I lost about 15 pounds in the first few weeks of doing this."

Interestingly enough, though, her powers increase when she is emotionally upset. She discovered her abilities one day after receiving a phone call saying that her grandmother was seriously ill. As she reached out for a small plastic bottle, it skidded away. After her grandmother's funeral, she tried it again, and was able to make the bottle move at will. She had been trying to move tiny objects before this incident—after seeing the Kulagina films—but without success. Yet her attempts had somehow awakened her latent powers, which were suddenly increased by the shock of her grandmother's illness.

How many other people would spend 15 minutes concentrating so hard that they lose weight and leave themselves too exhausted to speak? The answer is, almost no one. Could this be why so few of us have any idea of our hidden psychic potential?

Getting to Know Geller

The author and the enigma: Colin Wilson and Uri Geller in the course of their conversations during a visit to Barcelona, Spain.

"How do you feel about the idea of doing a biography of Uri Geller?"

The question was put to me by my literary agent in the spring of 1974. I said I thought it was a lousy idea. I had just read Puharich's book, and found it baffling and infuriating. But he seemed to have picked the bones pretty clean. Anyway, how much of a biography can you write of someone in his mid-20s?

Geller, it seemed, was under some kind of contract to the business tycoon Robert Stigwood, who was responsible for such shows as *Hair* and *Jesus Christ Superstar*. And Stigwood, it seemed, had decided to

"He bent a spoon, broke one of my keys, made my watch go back several hours..."

produce a film based on Uri's autobiography. Since I had written novels, biographies, and a book on the occult, I was apparently high on the list of possible biographers.

The film business is like a game of tennis, in which the original idea is batted back and forth 100 times or so, and the rules are changed every five minutes. While I was still brooding on the question of whether I could afford to turn down so much money, somebody else was asked to write the biography, and I was asked to turn in my own ideas for the film script. As a preliminary step, I was to meet Uri Geller for lunch.

I had no fixed ideas about Geller. I had seen him on television and thought him a personable young man, although hampered by a kind of exuberant immodesty. I also felt a certain sympathy for his struggles against the antisuccess mechanism, which was already gathering force. I had been through the same kind of thing myself in the mid-1950s, when my first book earned me the misleading label "Angry Young Man," and all the zany publicity that went with it. Within weeks, the same journalists who had launched myself and other "AYMs" (such as playwrights John Osborne and Brendan Behan) were tearing us to pieces. Now, as I heard Geller described as a materialist, a publicity-hound, and a downright fraud, my sympathies naturally tended to be on his side. As to whether he cheated or not, that was a matter on which I kept an open mind. But I had no doubt whatsoever that such powers as he had demonstrated on TV *could* be genuine; researching a massive book on the occult had convinced me of that.

That first lunch with Uri was an oddly disappointing and inconclusive affair. Mark Twain has a story about an inventor who asks a millionaire to finance an invention. Within five minutes, the millionaire is convinced, and takes out his checkbook. The inventor goes on to describe the benefits his invention will bring to society, and the millionaire begins to wilt and puts away his checkbook. And when the inventor goes on to detail the blessings his invention will bring to the whole world, the millionaire kicks him out. Uri has the same tendency to oversell himself. His steadily mounting enthusiasm seems an attempt to pressure you into belief, although his feats speak quite eloquently enough for themselves. On that first occasion he bent a spoon, broke one of my keys, made my watch go back several hours by clenching his fist above it, and read my mind. Only this last feat seemed 100 percent free of any suspicion of cheating. I sat with my back to a blank wall, and Mrs. Rae Knight, one of Stigwood's assistants, sat next to me. Uri, alone, sat opposite us, his back to the room. While I did my drawing—of a kind of spook—he turned his chair around and sat with his back to me. I cannot swear that he did not glance back over his shoulder, but Rae Knight, sitting next to me, could watch him all the time. Then I covered the drawing with my hand and Uri turned around. It took him several minutes to get it, and I had to concentrate hard. I may have made involuntary movements of my head as I tried to transmit the drawing, but hardly enough to tell him it was a face. The only possibility of cheating was that Rae Knight was some kind of accomplice; subsequent acquaintance with her has convinced me that nothing is less likely.

Randi could—and did—duplicate the spoon bending and watch altering, but not the mind reading (at least, not over the dinner table with me).

When I left Uri that day, I was puzzled and disturbed. I was more than half inclined to believe in his total genuineness. Yet he had placed a coin over the face of my watch before clenching his fist over it; Randi could quite easily have changed the hands in the split second before he placed the coin over it. Uri had taken my key across the room to a radiator, explaining that he gains power from metals; he could have bent it somehow as he crossed the room. (I did not go with him.) Added to these purely practical misgivings was my instinctive wariness of someone so prone to overselling his powers. So I was not really disappointed when, after a few months of silence, Rae Knight phoned me to say that the film seemed to be off.

I had reckoned without Uri. The next development in the story came to me via Rae Knight. She told me that Robert Stigwood had invited Uri to dinner at his house, to explain that the film idea was impracticable for the moment. Uri, who likes to get his own way, was incensed. As the butler served drinks from a large pewter tray, the tray suddenly snapped in two. A large poker in the fireplace proceeded to bend. Stigwood went down to the kitchen, to inquire about the delay in serving dinner, and learned that forks and spoons were bending. Stigwood was sufficiently impressed to reverse his decision on the film.

My next encounter with Uri was on "Start the Week," the BBC radio program I have already mentioned. Although the program is run by the gentle and courteous Richard Baker, I again had the feeling that Uri had been handed the wet end of the stick. He was introduced by Esther Rantzen, who read aloud a passage about bending keys and making watches change their time. A long dialogue followed, in which Uri clearly felt on the defensive. He took hold of a key belonging to Flora Rita Schreiber—author of *Sybil*, a book about multiple personality—and caused it to bend 10 degrees by rubbing it gently, allowing others to rest their hands on it at the same time. Someone suggested that he had borrowed the key before the program and bent it then; Miss Schreiber flatly denied that. At this point, Esther Rantzen explained that the earlier extract she had read was not a description of Uri, but of the Amazing Randi, bending a key by professional expertise; she went on to quote Randi: "I am proud of my profession. In my view Uri Geller brings disgrace to the art I practice. Worse than that, he warps the thinking of the young generation of forming minds—that is unforgivable." "In other words," added Miss Rantzen, hurling the final brick, "the effect we saw achieved on the table this morning could have been sleight of hand."

Of course, there is no law—or even convention—that says an interviewer has to be kind to an interviewee. Still, in my own experience, it always produces a sense of betrayal to find you have been lured into an ambush. Whether you play it cool, fight back, or lose your temper, you can't win. Fortunately, at this point Uri was spared the necessity of reacting by having to leave to catch a train; I was left with a feeling that he had just about held his own.

Above: Robert Stigwood, who began as a pop star manager, was sufficiently impressed by Uri Geller's feats to plan a film about him.

For the next few months I wrestled with the movie outline. Screen tests showed that Uri tended to underact rather than overact, which is unusual for a beginner, and good news for his director; it is the overactors who are impossible to coach. My own problems were less easily solved. From the beginning, I had felt that a straight film biography of Uri was a nonstarter; the idea of a film biography of someone who bends spoons is absurd. What is interesting about Uri is the *implications* of what he is doing. Where do his powers come from? Do we all have them? Are they just an accident, like double-jointedness, or are they connected to some inner development? It was this last question that interested me, and I played with the idea of a kind of "*2001* of inner space."

At the same time, I did my best to arrive at some more definite conclusions about Uri. Here, I was slightly more successful. I questioned a number of people who had seen him in action, and whose honesty I could trust. These included a number of publishers of my acquaintance, who had met Uri at the Frankfurt Book Fair in the previous year. In my own experience, publishers tend to be among the most hard-headed and skeptical members of the population. All were predisposed to regard him as a clever conjurer. One described handing Uri a key, and then deliberately walking backward as Uri made his way across to a radiator (to "gain power"), refusing to take his eyes off the key. At the radiator, Uri rubbed it gently and bent it within seconds.

The most interesting story I heard was of the dinner at which Uri caused coffeepots and sugar bowls to crumple inward, merely by pointing his finger at them. One publisher remained unconvinced, or at least defiant. Uri held his hand above the man's gold cuff link, without touching it. The link parted, and fell on the tablecloth. When the publisher picked it up to put it on again, the bar holding the two halves together was missing. A thorough search of the table and floor failed to reveal it.

A similar session has been described in *Esquire* by a contributing editor, Dotson Rader. Geller touched a gold link bracelet he was wearing, and told Rader that he had received it from an older woman, which was correct. He pointed to Rader's watch: "That has an engraving under the watch. But not written to you." He removed the bracelet from Rader's wrist, apparently without touching the clasp; as he continued to retail accurate information about its donor, Rader realized that the saltcellar was moving of its own accord across the top of the table. Rader describes it graphically as looking like "a tiny bishop wearing a silver miter shuffling across a snowy field."

Such incidents, along with other testimony, convinced me that Uri undoubtedly possesses some weird power.

When I began to plan this book, there were a number of questions that I needed to ask him. Because Uri spends most of the time in Mexico and traveling around the world, and I live in Cornwall, England, it was not easy to arrange a meeting. Finally, in February 1976, I heard that he was due to visit Spain; I arranged to fly to Barcelona to talk with him.

With Uri, things seldom go as expected. The day before I left, he telephoned to explain that he could not come to Barcelona. In Madrid, the police had had to eject a man from the hotel after he

Right: Uri Geller—shots taken during a lengthy *Esquire* interview session. Geller's good looks, which made him a successful model in Israel at the beginning of his postarmy career, have appeared in countless newspapers and glossy magazines as the editorial writers try to say something sensible about the nature of his obviously remarkable powers.

Below: Geller with the author in a Barcelona hotel suite, trying a simple ESP experiment. It was not particularly successful, possibly because Geller was tense.

Bottom: the author with his tape recorder and Uri with pencil and paper discussing the nature of Geller's paranormal abilities.

tried to attack Uri; then he received death threats from Palestinian guerrillas. A performer on stage is highly vulnerable, and the Spanish police could hardly be expected to keep him permanently surrounded by a bodyguard. So Uri decided to cancel his performances in Barcelona. Instead, he would meet me the following weekend in San Sebastian. I decided not to tell him that two Spanish monarchs have been assassinated in San Sebastian.

I went to Barcelona anyway—by this time I had other appointments. The day after my arrival, Uri phoned again from Valencia. He had decided to leave Spain without further performances, but would come to Barcelona to see me after all. I hastened out to buy a tape recorder—having left my own at home—and went to meet him at the airport.

Legend has it that Uri travels with a vast retinue of people. In fact, he was accompanied only by Shipi, and by his secretary Trina, a quiet American girl.

Meeting Uri again, I was struck once more by his good looks and his athletic condition. He has not allowed the luxurious life to increase his weight. He does not drink, smokes only an occasional cigar, and eats sparingly and simply. Morning and evening, he lies on his back on the floor and raises his legs above his head 80 times. He explained that if he ceases to feel in the peak of health, his powers deteriorate.

As we make our way toward the taxis, Uri speaks about the

death threats. "It is absurd. I have nothing against the Palestinians. All I want to see is peace in the Middle East." And he mentions his ambition to be invited to lecture in Egypt. I am again struck by the seriousness and enthusiasm with which he says everything; it may be a habit he has picked up from being interviewed so many times. He makes an impact of great sincerity, as well as charm. When you are talking with him, it is difficult to doubt him. And when he assures me, with great emphasis, "I have *never* cheated, never once in my life," I decide that he is probably speaking the truth.

As we speed along the road to Barcelona, there is a thud, and Uri looks around, alarmed, in case a suitcase has fallen off the roof. The driver pulls over to the side of the road and gets out. The luggage rack has become loose. As he tightens it, Uri asks him in passable Spanish, "Has this ever happened before?" The man says "No." Uri turns to me: "You see, these strange things are always happening around me. Of course, sometimes it is just coincidence. . . ." Five minutes later, the other side of the rack comes loose and we have to tighten that; Uri shakes his head but doesn't press his point.

Because I am here to ask him straight questions, I start off with the one that bothers me most. He seems to me altogether too preoccupied by the doubters and critics; and this, in turn, seems to be part of his overpreoccupation with material success. He was once reported as saying that his immediate ambition was to have a million dollars in the bank.

With his usual emphasis and sincerity, he says: "Let me explain. I think of my life as having three stages. In the first stage, I simply wanted to get known—I performed anywhere, all over Israel, sometimes for no fees. But my family needs money. So does Shipi's family. So the second stage is to make enough money to be able to live comfortably. In a short time—perhaps a year, perhaps more—I begin the third stage: to develop myself, to learn about my powers."

I ask him again what he thinks about the nature of these powers, but he shakes his head. "I just don't know. I don't know where they come from or what they mean, or why it should be me and not somebody else."

I present my own view: that they come from his own subconscious mind, and are of the same nature as poltergeist mani-

Right: Geller with two of his closest friends, the pianist Byron Janis and his wife Maria. Geller told the author about a strange poltergeistlike episode when a death mask of Chopin hanging in the pianist's apartment suddenly began to shed tears.

National Enquirer

Above: Geller with a bent spoon. He reports that often when he is most eager to bend metal he has no success, and then when he relaxes and puts it down, the spoon will "spontaneously" bend.

Above right: Felicia Parise, an American medical researcher who was so inspired by a film of the Soviet psychic Nina Kulagina that she determined to develop the power of moving objects simply by staring at them herself. After a period of intense concentration, she succeeded at last— but only when she stopped trying.

festations. He is clearly unconvinced. "I find that hard to believe because whatever lies behind these powers seems to be intelligent. Sometimes it plays jokes. In my book I say that maybe it's a Cosmic Clown."

He has a point. Poltergeists do sometimes behave intelligently —such as the one that wrote: "Esther Cox, you are mine to kill." And it would be absurd to rule out the possibility that there are intelligent forces, quite apart from man's own mind, that cause many so-called "psychic manifestations." Yet until we have some proof—or at least, some definite indication or clue—it is surely better to stick to the more plausible hypothesis.

In Uri's room, we switch on the tape recorder, and I continue down my list of questions. It strikes me that in one way Uri is unique among psychics. Every other one I can think of has had some kind of contact with the "dead" or the "other world." I want to know if Uri has ever felt that he was in contact with the dead. Uri slightly misunderstands my question, and proceeds to tell me an anecdote about when he came out of the army. He brought a small plastic bomb home with him. Unable to resist the temptation, he went up to the roof of his mother's house at midnight, and hurled it into the graveyard opposite. There was a loud crash, and he went back downstairs, and to bed. Some time later he was awakened by a knock at the door. He hurried to the door—and found no one there. Five minutes later, the knocking

recurred. Again, there was no one there. When it happened a third time, Uri jumped onto his bed, and stared out of the window, which had a view of the door. There was no one. The next morning, he went into the cemetery, searching for signs of the explosion, but could find none. He concluded that the rappings had been made by a spirit, perhaps reproaching him for tossing explosives.

At Puharich's house in New York, Uri heard three loud bangs coming from the ceiling overhead. Puharich's late father, who had been bedridden before his death, used to summon Puharich by banging his cane three times on the floor.

Uri had two other experiences suggesting the presence of a spirit—in both cases, the composer Chopin. While he was visiting the pianist Byron Janis, a death mask of Chopin over the piano had begun to shed tears. And when he and Janis stood by Chopin's grave in Paris, a stone flew past their heads. (Uri has suggested that Janis may be a reincarnation of the composer.) Both of these occurrences may be examples of the poltergeist phenomena that Uri seems to produce, and so also, I suspect, was the knocking at his door after he threw the bomb into the graveyard. There have been many well-authenticated cases of pictures and statues—usually religious ones—shedding tears; like the stigmata of some saints, these effects seem to be due to some activity of the unconscious mind.

The knockings in Puharich's house may be a different kind of phenomenon altogether. Many investigators now hold the view that haunting ghosts—as opposed to single-appearance phantoms—are not evidence of some intelligence present but are a kind of "recording" imprinted on a place by strong emotions. The haunting may be purely electrical in nature. When someone who is sensitive to the vibrations enters the electrical field, he will see—or hear—the ghost. An insensitive person would not even notice it. When Uri heard the knockings, Puharich himself was in the room. Could it have been *he* whose mind was sensitive to the "field," and whose unconscious mind projected the knockings so that Uri could hear them too? It may be that Puharich's subconscious is quite as active, in its way, as Uri's, and was partly responsible for the strange phenomena we have been examining.

People who are able to see ghosts are often—perhaps always—able to dowse for water with a divining rod; the powers seem to be related. This led me to ask Uri about his own dowsing abilities. He has been employed by a large mineral corporation to try

Below: three photographs of Nina Kulagina causing a card and cigar holder to move inside a closed box. She has managed to move a great variety of material from metals and plastic to (as here) paper. During a PK session an analysis of her brain activity showed extreme activity in the visual area of her brain, and her heartbeat has been recorded at four times the normal rate.

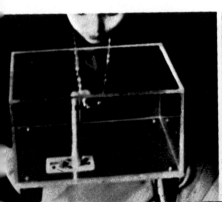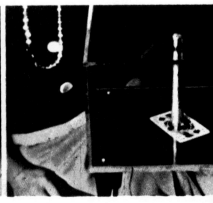

to locate mineral deposits from an airplane. "I can locate metals—tin, zinc, copper, gold, silver," he said, "but not oil or water. I tried it with them and it didn't work." Like Hurkos and Croiset, he has been able to apply his second sight to criminal cases. In one case, he entered the apartment of a kidnapped man, and then looked at a map of the city and indicated the area where he thought the man was being held. When the police flew him over the area in a helicopter, he was able to pinpoint the area even more accurately. "I just get a feeling when I'm close to what I'm looking for," he said. As it happened, the missing man was found, in the area specified by Uri, before the police had time to make use of his information.

When I asked Uri about this case, he seemed surprised, and a little alarmed, that I had heard about it, and asked me not to go into detail about it, or about other similar cases. I got the impression that this was not because he was afraid of criminal reprisal, but because he is not entirely happy about these powers. He seemed to have the same attitude when I asked about healing —for most dowsers also seem to be able to heal. In his autobiography he says that his few attempts at healing have been only minimally successful. I am inclined to wonder, again, whether he is afraid of being side-tracked into an area that at present holds no appeal for him. He seems to have decided that his abilities lie in certain directions; these are now well-tried and have brought him success. For the moment, that is enough.

Yet Uri himself—and this is perhaps the most interesting thing about him—is certain that psychic powers can be developed by anyone and are simply an extension of our normal powers. When he was a child, his own powers were restricted to reading his mother's mind, and causing watches to go forward or backward. In the period after he came out of the army he deliberately set out to extend them. "If you lift weights for a day or two, nothing happens. But if you lift weights every day for one or two years, then you will see the change." Most people, in his opinion, reveal no psychic powers because they fail to make any continuous effort to develop them.

He began to describe a simple exercise for developing such powers. "When you walk in the street, look at the next corner and try to see the color of the next car that will appear. *Keep practicing* this." We all possess powers of telepathy, he believes. For example, the déjà vu feeling—"I have been here before"—is due, he thinks to a kind of telepathy; your "thought waves" reach the place before you do, so you feel you have been there before.

These observations about effort seem to be confirmed by the experiences of Felicia Parise. Mrs. Parise's experiences raise another significant point, which Uri confirms. Her first experience of psychokinesis occurred spontaneously, when she was not making an effort. Uri mentions that this frequently happens to him. He tries hard to make a spoon bend; nothing happens. He relaxes and puts it down, and the spoon proceeds to bend. It may be that our violent efforts of will somehow frustrate themselves. When we relax, some deeper will takes over, and does the work effortlessly.

This applies also to his thought reading. In the three days we were in Barcelona, we made several attempts at thought reading, but none was particularly successful. I could believe him when he said this was because he was tense. There are so many stories of his telepathic feats from unbiased witnesses that there can be no reasonable doubt that he possesses this ability to a remarkable degree. A woman friend told me that on two occasions he had suddenly told her things that startled her. On the first occasion, he spoke of her husband, who was dead, and described their marriage and relationship with astonishing accuracy. Skeptics will object that he might have learned about this by questioning her friends. But on the second occasion he surprised her by telling her that she was about to go to dinner with a man she liked, and then described the man in some detail. In a spirit of perversity, she deliberately contradicted everything Uri said. "He is several years older than you." "No, he's younger." "He is English." "No, he's African." But she admitted to me that he had been right on every count—even to giving the correct first letters of the man's two names. Uri had looked increasingly baffled as she continued to contradict him; he was certain that the mental clues he was picking up from her were correct.

This woman's reaction to Uri is worth mentioning because it is not untypical. The Geller charm is potent—particularly when he

is talking; but, as with most charismatic people, there is a certain aggressiveness in his magnetism. People tend to express their reservations—and irritations—when they are away from him. There is something very childlike and open about Uri, and like many exuberant children he sometimes displays signs of spoiltness, particularly when he gets tired or when life becomes too complicated. To be sure, the pressures he lives under are intense, and it would take a saint to remain permanently patient and calm in this glaring light of nonstop publicity. A strong element of basic "niceness" has seen him through so far.

An incident in Spain illustrated the Geller magnetism in action. While I was being interviewed on the local television in Barcelona, Uri was taken to meet the Spanish publisher Noguer, who publish *The New Library of the Supernatural* in Spanish. I had certain misgivings about his visit. The only book that has been published in Spanish about Uri is as negative and hostile as Randi's—its author, like Randi, is a professional magician. As a result, many intelligent Spaniards take it for granted that Uri is a fake whose only interest is making money. A few people in the publisher's office had read the book and were inclined to be skeptical about the Geller "phenomenon," if not downright hostile.

Seemingly oblivious of the negative vibrations, Uri talked for five minutes about promotion and advertising. Then, perhaps sensing lack of enthusiasm, he asked for a watch. One of the chief editorial advisers removed one from his wrist and handed it to him. Uri placed it, face down, in the hand of the firm's director, then clenched his fist over it several times, so that his knuckles cracked. (He has explained that the cracking noise is essential; when it is absent, nothing happens.) A few seconds later, the watch had gone back an hour. Those I questioned later insisted that Uri had no time to alter the hands manually before placing it in the director's hand. Uri was then offered another watch, but he rejected it because it was gold. He is never quite certain whether

Geller has been frank about the importance he places on achieving fame and fortune, and now as a celebrity he has the opportunity to meet and spend time with other world celebrities as diverse as Omar Sharif, Salvador Dali, Elton John, and Muhammad Ali.

the "powers" might overdo it and ruin the watch. Instead, he asked for a spoon. Everyone was watching keenly, recalling suggestions that he bends the spoon by hand, then holds it in such a way that the bend cannot be seen as he rubs it. But Uri held the spoon by its end, so that almost all of it was visible. He placed one foot against a metal radiator to "gain power." Then he gently massaged the handle. Within a few seconds, it began to bend as if the metal had turned to rubber. He handed it back to the director and pointed out that it was continuing to bend in his hand. In fact, it went on bending until the handle was almost U-shaped.

Skepticism vanished; and so did much of the latent hostility. Such a demonstration has the effect of clearing the air like a thunderstorm. Uri's supremely confident manner ceased to jar. A few hours later, I met most of those who had been present, over a late-night dinner. The curled spoon was handed around and examined with astonishment; the general feeling now seemed to be that Uri Geller was really an extraordinary young man.

The following morning, Uri and I were due for a lengthy photographic session. Before the photographer arrived, I took the opportunity to ask a few questions that had occurred to me in the night. I was still trying to get some clue about the source of his powers. I set the tape recorder going and asked:

"This is an indiscreet question but . . . you are a fairly highly sexed person. There's an occult tradition called Tantrism that makes deliberate use of sexual energy. Do you think there could be any connection between your powers and your sexual energies?"

Uri was unoffended. "Strangely enough . . . I never asked people how they respond sexually. . . . But I think, according to the women I am with, or the girls I'm with, that I am more sensual than the ordinary person. . . . Yes, so maybe that has something to do with it."

The question was, I think, worth raising, even though Uri holds no definite views on it. Many investigators have observed the connection between sex and psychic force; Harry Price once interviewed the husband of a young Austrian medium, who told him that in the early days of their married life, ornaments would jump off the shelf when his wife had an orgasm. The young German office worker Anne-Marie ceased to cause poltergeist phenomena when she married. Esther Cox's manifestations were connected with a sexual trauma. So, according to Nandor Fodor, were those of "Mrs. Forbes." It is worth bearing in mind at least the possibility that Uri's powers may be, to some extent, sexual in origin.

There was one more question that I wanted to ask. Ever since I discovered, to my own astonishment, that I appear to be able to dowse, I have been brooding on the strange implications of the force that causes a forked whalebone rod to twist upward or downward in my hands. For me, the rod dips for water, and twists upward in the vicinity of ancient stones—of which we have hundreds in Cornwall, where I live. It seems to me that some electrical force from under the earth somehow affects the rod, through the medium of my brain. There is nothing very strange in this; we know the earth is an enormous magnet. If I hold the rod very tight, keeping the ends rigid, it still bends upward. Is it not conceivable, therefore, that the power that enables Uri to bend a spoon may be the power that twists the divining rod? And that his powers may come from the earth itself?

The idea excited Uri: "Isn't that strange?" he exclaimed. "I can use my powers much more strongly in Mexico. And in Israel. My body changes when I'm in these places. For some reason, I feel more fit, my skin gets tighter, my powers are stronger. . . . America is more difficult. My powers are low on the East Coast, and get stronger as I go west. In Africa my powers were stronger. Most of my failures were in Europe, and my biggest successes were in Australia, New Zealand, Africa, Mexico. . . . I was so powerful in Mexico. I could *feel* it. I stayed in the pyramids for four days, just walking around. In one moment, I seemed to see the whole scene that happened thousands of years ago, right there in front of me." The subject of Mexico deflected him from this theme. He went on to describe how when he arrived at the airport, there were five limousines waiting to meet him—one for each of his party, and two for the baggage. Once again, Uri was the delighted small boy, hobnobbing with presidents, loving every minute of his fame.

The photographer and his assistants arrived, and we went up to Uri's suite. I entered first. As I did so, there was a pinging noise, and Uri turned, saying "What was that?" An electric light bulb lay on the floor behind him. He snatched it up. "What's this?" He looked up at the light overhead; its bulb was still in. "It's an apport!" At that moment, the assistants came in; they included an American girl who was living in Spain. Uri showed them the bulb. "Look, it just fell from the ceiling." The girl volunteered the information that a bulb had fallen out of its socket in her apartment a week before. Uri became very excited and turned to me. "You see, things like this often happen to people just before they meet me. Didn't I tell you that? It happened to the Marquess of Bath. . . ." He told the girl he believed the bulb he had just found came from her house, and asked her if she could phone her home and find out if there was a bulb missing. She said the place was empty at that time, but that she could phone her husband during the lunch hour. It seemed to me that Uri was making a great deal of fuss over nothing, and I again had the feeling that he was pushing things a little too hard. Yet the sequel seemed to justify his excitement. The girl called her husband, who verified that a bulb *was* missing—from the same socket that had been involved in the earlier incident.

Below: the author as the subject of one of the "thought-pressure" experiments with Uri and his friends in a Barcelona hotel.

For the next half-hour or so, we submitted to being photographed. Uri wanted to demonstrate the "lifting experiment" on me. I had seen it done before; sometimes it had worked, sometimes not. This time, under Uri's direction, it worked beautifully. I sat down, and Uri, Shipi, Trina, and another woman tried to lift me by placing their index fingers under my armpits and knees. Naturally, it was impossible. Next, under Uri's instructions, they stacked their hands above my head, in such a way that no person's two hands were next to one another. Then, on a command from Uri, all removed their hands, replaced the index fingers under my arms and knees, and I sailed up easily into the air. It is a not uncommon feat, which can be performed by five people in any

Above: another try at the ESP game. The person in the center shuts her eyes and the four in the circle place their fingers very lightly on her shoulders, and (having decided together in advance on a single direction) all concentrate on influencing her to move in that direction.

place. Yet I have never seen it work quite so well as it did on the occasion when I tried it with Uri.

Next, at my suggestion, we tried an experiment in "thought pressure"—another party trick. One person stands in the center of a group of four, his eyes closed. The four place their fingertips very lightly on his chest and shoulders. Then, having decided tacitly which direction he should move in, they concentrate on making him sway in that direction. This, too, is an experiment that sometimes works and sometimes does not. In this case, we had a 75 percent success rate. Trina instantly swayed in the direction we wanted; so did Uri. So did I, when I took my place in the middle. Shipi swayed forward instead of sideways, as we had mentally directed him, although he said he felt a force impelling him in both directions.

There may be natural explanations for both of these feats. After all, it should theoretically be possible for four people to lift one person, even with their index fingers. It is possible that, after placing their hands in a pile (according to Uri, the hands should not be touching), they simply make a sudden concerted effort, which, perhaps for psychological reasons, they may not have made the first time. I find the thought pressure experiment harder to explain, simply because in my own experience there is definitely a sensation of being pulled or pushed in the required direction.

I myself am inclined to take the view, which Uri shares, that when several minds act in concert strange things can happen. He believes that this explains the remarkable success of his public experiments in spoon bending and watch repairing. The most recent had taken place only a couple of weeks before I saw him in Spain; a women's magazine asked its readers to concentrate at a certain time on a certain afternoon, and to get out any watches that needed repairing. There had been the usual overwhelming response from readers who claimed that long-inactive watches had started and that cutlery had bent. (A Swedish woman tried suing Uri because she claimed that one such experiment had bent her internal contraceptive coil and caused her to become pregnant.) The wife of screen writer Jesse Lasky later told me that she had taken part in the experiment, and that a clock that had been rejected by a local watchmaker as un-repairable started up and ran for 40 minutes.

It was nearly time for me to catch my plane back to London. I went up to my room to collect my bags; Uri volunteered to come with me. On the stairs, there was a loud pinging noise, and we turned to see a broken spoon on the stair carpet. "Another apport!" Uri shouted, in wild excitement, and yelled downstairs for the others to come and see. It was the lower half of a spoon. Yet again, I was puzzled and not entirely happy. If it had fallen out of the air in front of me, *that* would have been convincing. But its falling behind Uri was a different matter. He could quite easily have tossed it there, as he could have tossed the bulb earlier. He was walking behind me on both occasions. Yet why should he? I didn't need convincing. If anything, these ambiguous demonstrations tend to increase one's skepticism.

Half an hour earlier, Uri had said something that struck me as highly relevant to this whole problem. He emphasized how often his powers refuse to work in front of cameras, and how frustrating he finds it that some of his most convincing demonstrations happen when the camera is pointing in another direction. He said gloomily: "The things that always seem to work are the things that any magician can duplicate. Randi's quite right to point that out. But that's not because I'm doing a conjuring trick. You'd think—" He looked up suddenly. "You'd think that whatever causes these things to happen doesn't *want* them to be proved."

This is an observation that struck me years ago, when I was conducting my first lengthy investigation into the whole field of the occult. I began with a strong bias toward skepticism. Besides, to tell the truth, I still find occult phenomena a little preposterous and irrelevant. What do they really matter if you place them in the balance against the truly great human achievements—against the creative genius of a Michelangelo, a Beethoven, an Einstein? In that context they seem almost trivial. Yet unbiased investigation led me to conclude that paranormal phenomena are not pure wishful thinking; some of the evidence for telepathy, psychokinesis, out-of-the-body experiences, and reincarnation is highly convincing. So why do we not take it for granted, as we take for granted cosmic rays and neutron stars and subatomic particles, and many other things that we can never test with our own eyes? And the answer seems to be that the paranormal is oddly shy. Like a modest girl, it will show just so much of itself, and no more.

There is certainly enough evidence to convince those who are predisposed to believe, and also those who are genuinely open-minded. There is far from enough to change the mind of a determined skeptic. It tempts one to believe that some intelligent power is determined to keep us uncertain. The Daniel Dunglas Homes and Uri Gellers and Matthew Mannings are enough to make everybody reexamine their preconceptions about the universe and to undermine their complacencies. But no amount of investigation of their phenomena seems to provide us with the certainty we crave. The great breakthrough that science has accustomed us to expect never seems to come. And when an unusually gifted psychic such as Uri turns up and demonstrates his powers in the laboratory, he also has to be a born showman, with the personal mannerisms of a pop star, so that the skeptics can grimace and say: "What, *him*. . . ?"

These were the thoughts that occupied my mind as I wandered around a Barcelona park with Uri and observed his temper fraying as the cameraman demanded new poses, and the children trotted up to him with their autograph books. In my pocket, I had the half of a spoon that had fallen on the stairs behind us. Had he thrown it? On the whole, I thought not. Then who—or what—had? And why had it done so in such a manner as to leave room for doubt in my mind? As I stared into Uri's eyes—at the request of the cameraman—my instinct told me he was honest. So why were the "powers"—whether from starship *Spectra* or from his own subconscious—revealing themselves so enigmatically?

I find myself envying the total skeptics. They have such an easy way out.

Above: Geller and his friends try to lift the author into the air, using only their fingertips. They begin by trying to lift him that way, and of course fail. Then they stack their hands above his head, so that no person has his own two hands placed together.

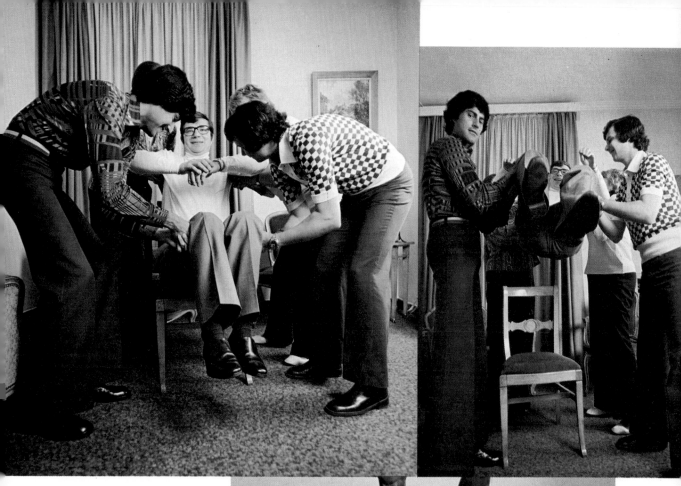

Above: on a command from Geller, everyone replaces their index fingers under Wilson's arms and knees.

Above right: immediately the author begins to rise in the air.

Right: Wilson sails up and away.

What Does It All Mean?

One cold winter morning in 1825, a five-year-old boy was taking a walk with his father. Suddenly he asked, "What hour was I born?"

"Four o'clock in the morning."

"What time is it now?"

"Seven fifty."

A few minutes later, the child said, "In that case, I'm now 188,352,000 seconds old."

His father noted down the number. When they got home, he did the calculation on a sheet of paper, and told his son, "I'm afraid you were 172,800 seconds wrong." "No," said the boy, "You've left out two days for the two leap years 1820 and 1824."

Was the child some great, universally

Millions of people have watched Geller bend thousands of spoons, forks, and miscellaneous cutlery, he has been tested in scientific laboratories, and still nobody knows exactly how it is done. Right: a sequence of stills taken from a movie showing Uri holding a fork (verified as being intact at the beginning by James Bolen, the photographer), which gradually becomes pliable, bends, and finally snaps into two pieces.

123

"There are vast areas within the brain about which we know nothing"

acclaimed genius, like Newton or Einstein? No, he was Benjamin Blyth, son of an engineer, and his name is otherwise unknown. Children with this peculiar power to calculate immense numbers are by no means a rare phenomenon. Most of them lose this power when they enter their teens.

The baffling thing about such prodigies is that there is no good reason why the human brain should possess such extraordinary potential. Scientists tell us that we developed from primitive fishes, which turned into reptiles, then into mammals. Man's remote ancestors came down from trees, survived the era of upheaval and drought known as the Pleistocene Age, and learned to live together in communities for their own protection. Man's brain developed as an instrument of survival, like his hands and his teeth. Why, then, should it be capable of such incredible feats of calculation, beyond anything he can ever have needed? It is as extraordinary as if, like some super-flea, he could leap 500 feet into the air.

This kind of puzzle is not confined to the human species. Birute Galdikas-Brindamour, a naturalist who has closely observed orang-utans in their natural environment, and who has brought up baby orangs, observes that they seem to possess an intelligence far in excess of the needs of their forest environment. Recent observation has revealed that even the shark is more intelligent than—according to the theory of evolution—it ought to be. For 300 million years this creature has remained unchanged, perfectly adapted to its environment, with senses that automatically guide it to food. With no choices to make, and no natural enemies, the shark does not *need* intelligence. Yet when tested for intelligence in laboratory mazes, the shark proves to have intelligence equal to that of a rabbit—a far more highly evolved form of life, which has plenty of natural enemies and therefore a greater need for intelligence.

Obviously the key to this mystery lies in the brain itself. Textbooks on the brain admit that there are vast areas within it about which we know nothing. Some physiologists have suggested that man uses only about one tenth of his brain. What is the purpose of the other nine tenths? No one seems to know. Presumably these other parts must have a purpose, or they would not have evolved. Is it conceivable that they govern faculties for which we no longer have any use? Most animal lovers can tell some story about the "second sight" of their pets, of a dog bristling and whining when forced to enter a room in which some tragedy has taken place, of a cat that knows when its owner has died, even though he or she is in a foreign country. The archaeologist and dowser T. C. Lethbridge observed that his cat would respond to other animals, such as mice and voles, which it could not see or hear because they were on the other side of a thick wall. And it is now widely believed that the mysterious homing instinct of animals and birds may be some kind of sensitivity to the magnetic forces of the earth—those same forces to which the dowser's rod responds. Animals seem to be more telepathic than human beings. So it is a reasonable assumption that these faculties may also be connected with the unknown nine tenths of the brain. Human beings no longer need for survival a "homing instinct" or a "second sight" to warn them of the

Right: a cross section of the human brain. Although certain areas of the brain have been identified as to the function controlled, it is still true that science knows nothing about vast areas of the brain, and any explanation of their function is still hypothesis.

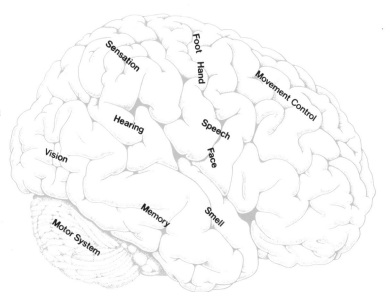

Below: an orang-utan leaning on a stick in its forest home. Studies of baby orang-utans reared away from the natural environment seem to show that the animals possess intelligence far in excess of their natural needs.

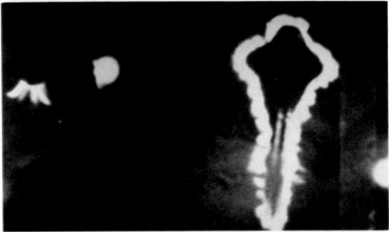

Above: Geller drawing his forces
together in intense concentration.
Casual observers, dazzled by his
superb showmanship, often overlook
the effort involved, which—as
Uri admits—sometimes interferes
with achieving the desired result.

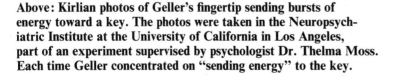

Above: Kirlian photos of Geller's fingertip sending bursts of
energy toward a key. The photos were taken in the Neuropsych-
iatric Institute at the University of California in Los Angeles,
part of an experiment supervised by psychologist Dr. Thelma Moss.
Each time Geller concentrated on "sending energy" to the key.

Right: a close-up showing Uri's fingerpad, with the energy spurt.

approach of enemies. Therefore, in most of us these faculties lie dormant.

All of which should certainly help us to understand Uri Geller's ability to read minds. Something has awakened his dormant faculty. But what about his power over metals?

Here we have to consider another possibility. In an important essay called "The Energies of Man," the psychologist William James talked about the phenomenon of "second wind"—how we can apparently be exhausted, and then quite suddenly seem to switch over to a "reserve energy tank" and feel completely refreshed. He speaks of the case of a colonel during the Indian Mutiny who was in charge of a besieged garrison with many women and children under his care, and who went for an entire week without sleep, living on brandy. He never became drunk, and it did him no harm; the emergency called upon his vital reserves. James concludes that we all possess immense "vital reserves" that we seldom use because we are habit bound and allow ourselves to become easily fatigued.

In speaking about Uri Geller and other similar cases, Professor John Taylor has also discussed these vital reserves—for example, how a frantic mother has been known to lift a heavy vehicle from her child, who was trapped under it. He concludes that the muscles themselves probably store up the immense energies required for such feats. This, he thinks, might explain the energies involved in poltergeist activity, and possibly in Uri Geller's metal bending.

This is an interesting and plausible idea, but it contains one pitfall. When we think of the human body or brain as a kind of

Above: Thelma Moss, who has taken more Kirlian photographs and done more experimental work with them than anyone outside Russia. She reported that her informal experiments with Geller appeared to have been very successful, but were not tightly enough controlled for her to exclude the possibility of deliberate fraud by Geller.

Right: experiments—using the Kirlian technique on color film—in which Geller was attempting to send a shape telepathically.

Below: in this photo, Geller was trying to form the shape of the number 5, which he felt he was then receiving telepathically.

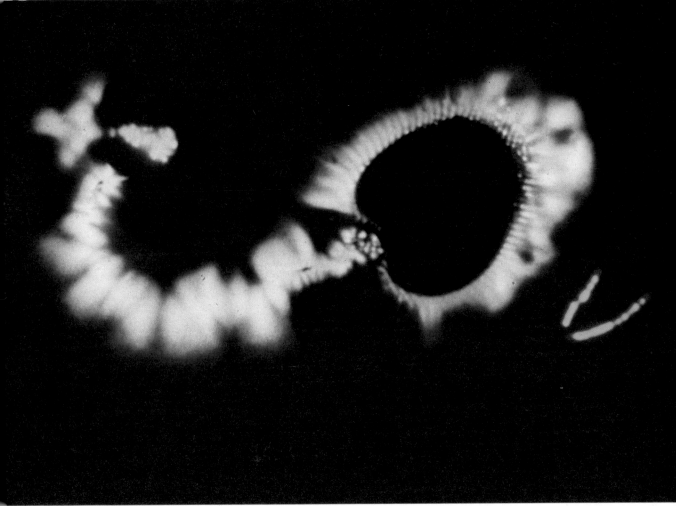

battery that stores energy, we are thinking in exclusively physical terms. But when the colonel lived for a week on brandy, he was *creating* energy, burning up surplus fat, converting the alcohol to "fuel." When Felicia Parise tries to move a glass by the power of her mind, she perspires heavily and loses weight—she is creating energy out of mass. Yet, oddly enough, she first succeeded in moving an object by mind power when she was not trying. Uri Geller has frequently made the same observation: that a spoon may remain unbent while he tries hard to bend it, then start bending when he puts it down and thinks of something else. The logical inference is that the energy used in these poltergeist-type activities is not ordinary muscular energy, but some other kind, that we are less able to control. It is analogous to the situation in which you try hard to remember something—for example, a name—but fail totally while you keep trying; then, as soon as you think of something else, the name comes to you. Your brain was doing its best to obey your command, but you were somehow blocking its proper activity by summoning crude will power.

The picture that begins to emerge is a complex one. It begins to look as if both the brain and the body have great untapped resources, including the ability to create vital energies at short notice. But the energies involved in psychic activities are not the energies we normally use, so most of us have some difficulty in calling on them. Certain people, like Uri, are able to do so—just as some children can calculate enormous numbers.

Uri's powers may have originated in the sewing machine incident, when he received an electric shock. At least, it seems significant that he "draws power" from both metal and water, the two substances that conduct electricity.

The expression "draws power" suggests another possibility. The earth is an enormous magnet. The ancient Chinese believed that lines of force run across the landscape. They called them "dragon paths" and built their temples on them. In England, students of the countryside have observed how many ancient stone circles and monuments seemed to be built on similar alignments, and how certain religious centers, such as Salisbury and Glastonbury, seem to be the meeting place of several such lines. There is some evidence that these "ley lines" correspond to natural lines of force in the earth. They certainly respond very powerfully to the divining rod, which suggests that there is some form of interaction between the dowser's brain—whose activity the divining rod "meters"—and the force he is tuning in to. Some dowsers, such as T. C. Lethbridge, are so sensitive that they experience a kind of electric shock, like mild static, when they place their hand on ancient stone monuments.

If Uri derives power from a metal radiator—which is presumably earthed, or grounded—there is at least a reasonable possibility that the power he is using comes from the earth. It may seem to be a contradiction that his powers are stronger in airplanes; but then, as everyone knows, the lines of force in a magnet run around it from one pole to the other; in an airplane Uri could have been in the center of the force field. (It would be interesting to see how his powers would operate if he actually stood on the north or south magnetic pole.)

Above: two of the first Kirlian photographs taken of Geller. In the top picture, his finger is at rest. In the bottom one, he is sending energy toward a watch.

129

Left: an early practitioner of the strange art of hypnotism, in the traditional pose that has since become a hallmark of the stage hypnotist capturing his subject.

Right: a caricature of Mesmer's healing salon, with the tub that contained water and magnetized iron filings, which was believed to serve as the focus for cures.

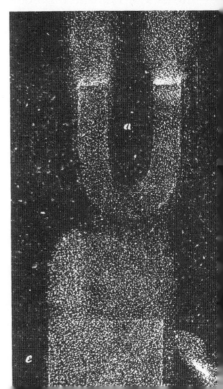

It is also worth bearing in mind that occultists have always held the view that magnets possess peculiar properties. This seemed to be given scientific backing in the 1770s, when Franz Anton Mesmer, the discoverer of "mesmerism" (now called *hypnotism*), declared that he had been able to cure sick people by stroking them with magnets. Within 10 years, scientists had decided that Mesmer was a charlatan, and he died an embittered old man. In the 1840s another scientist, Baron Karl von Reichenbach, discovered that his patients were not only sensitive to magnets but also able to see colors streaming from the two poles. In one experiment an assistant in the next room uncovered the poles of a huge magnet, and a patient lying in bed—and observed by Reichenbach—instantly detected the magnetism as a tingling sensation. When the patient was unconscious, her hand would stick to a magnet as if it were metal. Reichenbach believed he had discovered some unknown energy, which he called "odic force"; he said that is could also be detected streaming from the ends of the fingers. Again, it took only a few years for scientists to decide that he was a crank, and that human beings cannot be influenced by magnets. Yet now, in the second half of the 20th century, investigators believe they have discovered a method of photographing this "aura" that streams from the ends of the fingers. The technique is known as Kirlian photography, and it is under systematic investigation in various laboratories. Could Reichenbach also have been correct about magnets? Is it possible that certain human beings may be sensitive to magnetic forces of the earth? If so, then we have one more vital clue to the mystery of Geller's powers.

The real problem, as we try to explain the feats of a Daniel Dunglas Home or Uri Geller or Matthew Manning, is that we lack a firm theoretical foundation. The philosophers of ancient Greece were highly intelligent men, but all their attempts to explain lightning were a waste of time, because they had never heard of electricity. In fact, no one was in a position to understand lightning until Benjamin Franklin literally brought it down

to earth in 1752 by flying a kite with a wire cord in a thunderstorm. Poltergeist activities can leave us in no possible doubt that we are dealing with some unknown force that does not obey the known laws of physics. If 100 years of psychical research have taught us anything, it is that the mind is able to ignore some of the laws of nature. For example, in our natural world, time flows onward, in the words of the hymn, "like an ever-rolling stream," and the future is hidden from us. Yet there are thousands of well-authenticated cases of people who have been able to glimpse the future, in dreams, in visions, or in waking consciousness.

If you were a worm, and were made to crawl across an enormous chessboard, you would soon begin to believe that one of the laws of nature is that black always follows white, and white

Left: an illustration from Baron Karl von Reichenback's *Le Fluide des Magnétiseurs*, summarizing his work in the 1840s Here a mysterious light appears at the magnetic points of the fingers and the magnet, which Reichenback called the "odic force."

Right: Mozart at the age of six, the archetypal example of the young prodigy—he composed a symphony when he was only eight years old—whose extraordinary powers did not fade as he grew up, but continued and developed in his adult years.

follows black. If someone explained to you that black does not follow white, or vice versa, and that they were both present at the same time, you would find it incomprehensible.

We human beings are accustomed to day following night, in a predictable order; and because, like the worm, we cannot see ahead, we believe this to be a law of nature. Yet the evidence of hundreds of prophets and seers seems to demonstrate otherwise; yesterday and today and tomorrow somehow exist simultaneously.

Another tale of mathematical genius may help us to understand this. In 1837, a 10-year-old Sicilian peasant boy was brought to Paris to be examined by great mathematicians; his name was Vito Mangiamele. The mathematician Arago asked him, "What satisfies the condition that its cube plus five times its square is equal to 42 times itself increased by 40?" It took Vito less than a minute to produce the correct answer: five.

Arago complained that the teachers of Vito Mangiamele had kept secret the methods he used to work out these problems. But if we think about it for a moment, we can see that this is absurd. Vito was not applying some simple formula to solve his problem. What he did was somehow to envisage the whole system, to see it whole in his mind's eye. If you or I try to work it out in our heads, we quickly realize that this is the trouble. We can't envisage it. As we struggle with one aspect of the problem, we forget all the others. Vito could see the whole problem as if it were a kind of drawing traced in the air, in three dimensions.

Imagine, for example, that someone drew a donkey's tail on a

blackboard, then its head, then its back, its belly and two front legs, and then asked: "What have I left out?" Any child could say: "Its hind legs." Yet if the same person only described the parts of the donkey verbally, it would be rather more difficult to pinpoint the missing part of its anatomy—particularly if you were a poor visualizer. For most of us, a mathematical problem is something to be dealt with in sequence; we relate the numbers to each other as we are directed by certain words such as "equals" and "times itself," using a linear process. But Vito was somehow able mentally to draw the problem in the air and see its parts, so that the unknown quantity, the missing part, was immediately obvious.

When we try to solve a problem of this kind we realize that the mind itself seems to be weighed down by a kind of gravity. We are like the worm on the chessboard. We may try to make our thought take wing; but except in rare moments it can only crawl on its belly. By some odd freak, Vito was free of this limitation—at least where mathematics was concerned.

The same thing seems to be true for people with powers of prophecy, of foreseeing the future. The gravitational force that holds most of us in the present moment seems to permit them to escape. They float up into the air like a balloon, and can see what lies ahead.

Most human beings cannot even begin to imagine a universe in which all events have already taken place. Yet the evidence of seers and prophets suggests that this is what the universe is really like. Time is a kind of illusion, produced by our worm's-eye view.

Above: George Parker Bidder, a stonemason's son born in 1806, who became famous as a calculating prodigy, answering (in about a minute) such queries as "Suppose a city to be illuminated with 9999 lamps, each lamp to consume 1 pint of oil every 4 hours, how many gallons of oil would they consume in 40 years?" The correct answer was 109,489,050 gallons.

Right: Viola Olerich, born in Iowa in 1897. As her "examination certificate" points out, before she was two she knew 2500 nouns.

The same may be true of other laws of nature. If Ingo Swann really visited Mercury in eight minutes, then space, like time, is also a kind of illusion. If poltergeists can make solid objects pass through walls, then the laws of matter are less rigid than we assumed.

Yet these suggestions still leave a great deal unexplained. Puharich's book, in particular, seems to defy all attempts at rationalization. But let us look at it a little more closely.

Most of the strange happenings described by Puharich conform to the pattern of poltergeist activity. Objects appear and disappear or fly through the air, metals crack or bend, items of furniture move of their own accord. But metallic voices speaking from a tape recorder, and sightings of flying saucers, are a different matter.

It is worth comparing Puharich's experiences with those of Jesse Lasky, the Hollywood screen writer. In October 1975, Jesse Lasky and his wife Pat went to a London bookshop where Uri was signing copies of *My Story*. Jesse introduced himself; Uri looked at him sharply and asked them to wait until after he had finished the book-signing session. After bending a woman's car key, Uri said, "Look at your keys, everybody." Pat opened her handbag and discovered that her door key was bent. Afterward, Uri returned with them to their apartment. He declined to bend a key, saying he was too tired, but when the Laskys' attractive daughter Lisa arrived, he seemed to be revitalized, and instantly bent a thick metal spoon, placing himself against a refrigerator door to draw power. On the second occasion when he visited their home, there was a pinging noise like a bullet, and an American Indian-style silver button bounced on the kitchen counter in front of Trina, Uri's secretary. It came from a card in Pat Lasky's bedroom drawer, three rooms away; Uri knew nothing of its existence and had not been into the room. At the time the button flew across the kitchen, he was standing with a bottle of milk in one hand and a tin of cocoa in the other. The drawer in the bedroom was found closed, and inside it was the card, with one button missing. They calculated the path of the button, and concluded that it had traveled through three walls.

(When I saw him in Barcelona, Uri told me that a television camera had actually filmed an apport—a watch—under laboratory conditions, and that when the film was projected in slow motion, it revealed that the watch appeared and disappeared several times as it fell through the air.)

A week before the Laskys met Uri, a lever in their fuse box disconnected itself seven times in quick succession; an electrician could find nothing wrong. An important book disappeared, then reappeared—after a search—under a chair that they had searched several times. One evening some months later, the lights of a house where they were staying continually turned on and off in an unaccountable manner. On the following morning they received a transatlantic phone call from Uri; and they suspected that these events might be related.

There would be no point in detailing the many other events that occurred during Uri's visits to the Laskys; they conform to the same pattern. There were no metallic voices, no messages from space.

It is interesting to speculate on why Uri "took" to the Laskys so quickly—in fact, on first meeting them. He took to Puharich in much the same way. The Laskys radiate an air of warmth and sympathy. Jesse, like Puharich, is a man in his 60s, something of a father figure. The Laskys had no doubt whatsoever about Uri's powers before they went to his book signing. Significantly, Jesse's account of their friendship begins: "In October of 1975, we felt a compulsion to see Uri in person. . . ." The word "compulsion" suggests that they felt literally drawn toward him. Moreover, Uri's powers seem to have been unusually active whenever he was in their company. We have already noted that his powers tend to "dry up" in front of a hostile audience; even my sympathetic but unpsychic presence seems to affect them adversely—as in the case of our unsuccessful telepathy attempts in Barcelona. On the other hand, certain people seem to stimulate his powers, as if their subconscious minds provide some kind of

Above: Geller with Jesse Lasky and his wife Pat, shown here wearing on a chain one of the keys bent by Geller—although in this particular case it was in her handbag at the time, and Uri had not actually touched it.

energy or support. Could this explain that immediate intimacy that sprang up between Uri and the Laskys?

Pat Lasky made an observation that may be relevant to Uri's powers. She normally diets fairly carefully, but while the Laskys were seeing Uri, this proved to be unnecessary. She ate what she liked and still lost weight. She commented that other people who have spent time with Uri have had the same experience. It is as if Uri is drawing energy from people with whom he establishes a certain rapport.

Assuming that a similar close rapport existed from the start between Uri and Puharich, and assuming that Puharich was already predisposed to regard Uri as a possible messenger from "the Nine," it hardly seems surprising that the incidents of their early acquaintance included messages from space and sightings of UFOs.

Of course, it is possible that a real, objective UFO did appear, as Puharich related in *Uri*. There are far too many sightings reported around the world to dismiss them all as illusion. Yet Puharich admits: "I recognize the possibility that there may not have been a spaceship there at all. I am aware that the three men in the command car saw nothing because there was nothing to see; I recognize that the three of us certainly had the image of a spaceship in our minds. . . ." That is to say, the spaceship could have been some kind of collective telepathic image.

The psychologist Carl Gustav Jung had an interesting suggestion about UFOs. He believed that they were neither real nor imaginary, but some kind of psychic projection of the human subconscious. In our materialistic age, he suggested, many people experience a longing for messianic visions. But UFOs may not be an "hallucination" in the ordinary sense; they might be seen by many people at the same time, some of them wholly skeptical or uninterested. A symbol from the "collective unconscious" would somehow, in such a case, find its way into the objective world. It would be real in somewhat the same sense as a picture projected onto a movie screen is real.

It seems clear that Puharich—if not Geller—has a tendency toward "messianic expectations." This reinforces the suspicion that he may have been as responsible as Uri for the curious events described in this book.

The word "magic" is frequently used in connection with Uri Geller, though never by respectable scientists. In some ways, it is not wholly inappropriate. Magic is basically a belief that the known laws of nature—of physics, in particular—are not the only laws of our universe, and that man can make use of a completely different set of laws. The concept of the "true will" is particularly important. In our everyday dealings with the physical world, we use a clumsy, physical kind of will. A scientist would say that wishful thinking could have no possible effect on the real world. Yet many people have had the experience of wanting something intensely, of directing the whole will toward it, and of eventually getting it, as if by the operation of some unknown law of attraction. The poet Robert Graves, for example, asserts that many young men use a kind of unconscious sorcery in seducing young women. This, say occultists, is the operation of the "true will," a deeper will than our ordinary state of volition.

Sometimes this true will operates on a purely physical level. William James cites the example of a football player who plays the game with technical expertise, but who one day seems to be carried away and achieves a strange perfection so that everything he does turns out right. Again, this is the true will in action.

Human beings are, on the whole, passive creatures: a little discouragement upsets us; a dull Monday morning depresses us; a few setbacks destroy our will to win. Yet the right kind of stimulus can call forth remarkable potentialities—as in the case of the colonel who lived on brandy during the siege, or that of a mother lifting a heavy vehicle off her child.

Great artists, great performers, great sportsmen, may spend years of discipline learning how to tap the power of true will, and so raise a technically brilliant performance to the level of genius. By contrast, some people seem to be born with the ability to contact the true will. Hitler struck people as rather ordinary in personal conversation; yet in front of an audience some extraordinary power seemed to emanate from him. Many religious leaders have possessed this power in a different form. If such men have not achieved their power by long and painful discipline, they may sometimes be dangerous—as in the case of Hitler.

Gifted psychics seem to form a subgroup within this category. They create an impression of freakishness. Reading of telepaths and mediums, one sometimes feels as if two lines in a telephone exchange have been accidentally crossed so that normal conversations get interrupted by unwelcome voices—or as if the insulation has worn away from an electric wire, so that unexpected short circuits occur. People under stress may become telepathic for a short period, Rudolf Steiner, the founder of the Anthroposophical Society, told a story of a German pilot in World War I who began to know in advance which of his companions would be killed on missions. This knowledge thoroughly unnerved him. Steiner advised him to drink wine; when he followed this prescription, the insights vanished. Significantly, Uri does not drink, because he feels this would damage his powers. Peter Hurkos, as we have seen, gained his powers of second sight after serious concussion. Uri's powers may originate in the electric shock he received as a child.

It may be significant that most normal human beings feel either bored or repelled by the thought of paranormal powers. If we examine the matter objectively, we have to admit that the powers of Daniel Dunglas Home or Eusapia Paladino are as undeniable as those of Mozart or Einstein. Yet we instinctively feel that the powers of Mozart and Einstein are important and relevant to us as human beings; those of Home and Paladino are unimportant and irrelevant.

If this is true, it suggests that humans may be intended, or programed by nature, to evolve along certain lines, and that such powers as communication with the dead, or thought reading, or metal bending, do not lie along the direct path of evolution. The occultist Aleister Crowley, sometimes called the "Great Beast," once said that the aim of the magician is to become a god. But if you asked most people to name a godlike human being, Crowley is the last name that would occur to them; they would be more likely to mention Michelangelo, Leonardo da Vinci, or

Right: Robert Leftwich, a noted
English dowser, who believes
he has simply developed latent
powers that many people might
possess if they wished to try.

Beethoven. True greatness, in the eyes of most thoughtful people,
is the spirit's attempt to transcend human triviality and self-
absorption.

This is one of the reasons why the majority of people are still
indifferent to psychic matters in general and to extraordinary
individuals such as Uri Geller in particular. But there is also a
less creditable reason. If you ask a roomful of people how many
believe in ghosts, most of them will say they do not; speak to
them individually, and most will admit the possibility. There is
a fear of being thought credulous, a desire to maintain a reputation for sturdy common sense.

Yet if the powers of a Peter Hurkos or Matthew Manning or
Uri Geller are genuine, they may be of considerable importance
to the development of the human race. Only a fool would reject
the assistance of something that could make his everyday life
easier and more agreeable. And there are many ways in which
we can make practical use of psychic powers. Uri Geller's ability
to dowse for metals from an airplane and Croiset's ability to
find missing people are rather spectacular examples of the use
of psychic powers. But there are hundreds of dowsers who, when
they lose something, do not spend hours searching for it, but
simply allow their dowsing rods or pendulums to guide them to
the missing object. There are hundreds of sensitives who can
diagnose an illness by laying their hands on the patient, or simply
looking at a sample of his handwriting. Andrija Puharich cites a
well-documented story of a workman who was buried when a
trench collapsed, and succeeded in sending a telepathic message

of his plight to a workmate at another site. I myself once used telepathy to locate my family, when we had become separated in a large park—by making my mind a blank and simply allowing my feet to take me to them. All these are examples of powers that most human beings could develop and utilize.

In most rural areas such powers are generally accepted; country doctors, for example, know that a wart charmer can remove warts more quickly and efficiently than they can with their scalpels and caustic soda. Whether this is due to suggestion or hypnosis is beside the point; it works. It would work equally well in cities, but the mental attitude of city-dwellers is somehow hostile to the idea. Accustomed to the use of all kinds of mechanical aids, they find the idea of "magic" disturbing and somehow irrelevant.

The problem is that humans have become machine-minded. Surrounded by complex technology, we have become passive in the face of our artificial existence. The passivity, the sense of helplessness, breeds neurosis that expresses itself in a variety of disturbing symptoms: urban guerrilla warfare, a soaring crime rate, and a worldwide drug problem. This collective neurosis is one reason for the occult revival and the current interest in all kinds of messiahs and gurus: many people feel that man ought to return to the task of finding himself.

In this sense, Geller may be a more relevant figure than most contemporary cult leaders. In insisting that anyone could develop the power to read minds and bend metal, he represents a healthy and sane individualism. His power over metal could be regarded as a symbol of the power of mind over the material from which all machines are made, just as his power over clocks seems to be a symbolic defiance of time. The skepticism he arouses is partly an emotional resistance to the challenge of developing one's own spiritual powers. Geller represents the belief that man is an altogether less passive and helpless creature than most of us assume. And he represents a flat denial of the current nightmare—dramatized so effectively in the film *2001, A Space Odyssey*—that man will one day be superseded by computers. For Geller, the computer remains the servant, one that can be immobilized or regalvanized by the curious powers of the subconscious mind. A civilization that accepted the powers and ideas of Uri Geller would be a great deal healthier than a civilization that accepts the gloomy predictions of every "scientific" futurologist.

The question of Uri's own future is an interesting one. When he left Israel for Germany in 1972, it must have seemed that his possibilities were endless. Yet the trajectory of his career continued to rise only for another 18 months; then the antisuccess mechanism began to operate. The problem was that he had become a household word. No psychic had ever achieved so much international publicity—not even Daniel Dunglas Home. The only "magician" of comparable celebrity was Houdini; and he made the sad discovery that he had to devise more and more sensational effects to hold public interest. This, unfortunately, is the law that governs notoriety. Uri's problem, therefore, has been to try to escape this vicious circle, and to find a new direction for development. But which direction?

Above: the "sleeping prophet" Edgar Cayce, who over a long period was apparently able to diagnose the illnesses of people not present, and clairvoyantly prescribe treatment, which—according to his patients—was often completely successful. Below: American psychic Jeane Dixon, who foretold the crash that killed Dag Hammerskjöld, then United Nations Secretary General, and predicted the assassination of President Kennedy.

Right: where does Uri Geller go from here? On the cover of his record is an artist's expressive interpretation of Geller's powers, the birth of a vigorous new force.

There are obviously a number of possibilities. The most straightforward would be close cooperation with scientists in an attempt to understand the source of his powers. Are they electrical or magnetic, or (as Professor John Taylor believes) in some way muscular? If they spring from his unconscious mind, could they be explored by modern techniques of depth psychology?

There is also the possibility of deliberately developing these powers. In his childhood, they were limited to reading his mother's mind and influencing watches. Later, he discovered that he could read other minds, and bend metals. More recently, he has developed powers of dowsing and psychometry, and even explored the possibility of healing. The episode of the moving saltcellar, witnessed by the *Esquire* reporter, also suggests that he may possess unusually strong powers of telekinesis of the type practiced by Felicia Parise, among others.

There is another possibility—one that holds great promise of self-fulfillment not only for Uri himself, but also for others. All major religious teachers have taught that man's powers, both physical and psychical, can be developed and controlled by discipline, and that the most effective disciplines are those that aim at control of his inner being. The philosopher Gurdjieff, who himself possessed remarkable psychic powers, taught that man consists of "personality" (the "outer man") and "essence" (the "inner man"). Psychic powers, he declared, are a mere by-product of the development of essence.

Geller recognizes the seriousness and importance of the challenge. He also recognizes that the development of his powers has so far proceeded in a rather haphazard way. In a life of constant travel and performances, he has had no opportunity to try to explore that inner space in which his powers probably originate. The next stage of his career, the stage of self-exploration, will provide him with that opportunity. When I spoke to him about it, he seemed both attracted and alarmed by the prospect.

What is clear is that Uri Geller is in an ideal position to test the truth of the assertion that psychic powers can be increased by inner discipline. In an age that has become obsessed with questions of the psyche and expansion of consciousness, he could help to provide the answers to some fundamental questions— and also, perhaps, become an important symbol of the search for self-knowledge and self-meaning.

Uri Geller

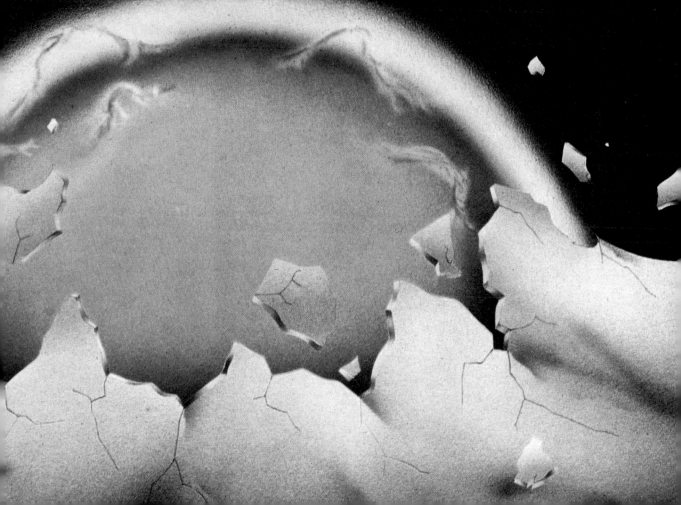

Index

References to illustrations are shown by italics.

Picture Credits